RENAL

COOKBOOK

FOR BEGINNERS

The Complete Guide to Low Sodium, Potassium and Phosphorus Recipes to Reduce Kidney Workload | 30-Day Kidney-Friendly Meal Plan to Avoid Dialysis

ADELINE KELLY

In this document you will find recipes that you can repeat for 2000 days

Contents:

INTRODUCTION

The Renal Diet will help to restore kidney function and help avoid complications in the future. This diet can be eaten on a daily basis. The Renal Diet will also help maintain a healthy heart. The Renal Diet changes how your body processes nutrients, reducing inflammation, improving circulation and healing your body from the inside out. This book will tell you everything you need to know about the Renal Diet.

You can eat delicious, flavorful, and healthy food if you have a renal diet. This cookbook will show you just how easy and delicious it can be to eat your ideal diet. This book is perfect for the person who wants to go on the renal diet for weight loss, the person with a kidney disease, or anyone else who wants to enjoy a healthy diet.

Being on a renal diet can be a tough challenge, but it can also be rewarding. This is because we are able to not only be healthier but live a better quality of life. In this book, you'll learn more about renal diet basics, its benefits and why it's important to start a renal diet. You'll also learn about the Renal Diet Recipes Cookbook and its benefits.

Kidney disease is not easy to deal with. Even if you are not living with kidney disease, there is still a chance that you might be diagnosed with it. It can be a difficult diagnosis to find the right diet to help your kidneys recover. That's why it's important to read more about kidney disease and the benefits of renal diet. This book discusses what the Renal Diet is and how it works.

Chapter 1: Fundamentals of Renal Diet

We are pleased to have you join us in perusing the Renal Diet Cookbook, which was put together by local dietitians specifically for people who suffer from chronic renal disease. After receiving feedback from a number of you indicating that you need further advice and assistance in order to adhere to your renal diet, we spent no time in putting together this recipe book in order to provide it to you. As a result, it is our sincere wish that this book will serve as a wellspring of encouragement for you at any stage of the therapeutic process.

Rather of focusing on lavish cuisine for evening get-togethers, the primary emphasis of this cookbook is placed on classic English dishes as well as recipes from other nations that have been included into the typical English eating pattern.

We are also aware that many of you may be adhering to a dietary restriction, wanting to become more active, or maybe needing to put on weight; hence, we have designed routines that are adaptable enough to match your requirements.

We hope that you are getting enough of the essential nutrients that you need from the meals that we are now providing for you, and that you are enjoying them.

If one follows a diet that is rich in certain nutrients, it may be able to reduce the risk of developing kidney disease and even improve kidney function in individuals who already have the condition. The renal diet that is ideal for you will depend on a number of factors, including the condition of your kidneys, the amount of physical activity you get, and any other health problems you may be dealing with at the time. Despite the fact that the renal diet that is ideal for you will vary depending on the condition of your kidneys, there are a few things that should always be kept in mind, as well as specific nutrients that you should either include in your diet or stay away from. In any event, food and nutrition may function as a form of therapy, and in this section, we will go through the advantages and disadvantages of each option. In discussions that pertain to kidney health and the renal diet, protein is often misinterpreted and given the wrong impression. Because your needs for protein shift depending on the amount of exercise you do, it is important to discuss this topic with your family physician.

If you have renal illness, you should generally cut down on the amount of protein you consume. However, there is conclusive evidence that protein is necessary for human health, and in the end, the decision comes down to personal preference. You may be able to acquire enough of the protein you need without placing an unnecessary strain on your kidneys and heart if you cut out dairy products and red meat products from your diet.

Although chicken is a healthier alternative than red meat, chicken that is farmed using traditional farming methods may sometimes include high levels of hormones; thus, organic chicken is the superior option. On the other hand, eating fatty fish, which is laden with healthy fats that are beneficial to both your kidneys and your general health, is an excellent method for obtaining the protein you need. Researchers have shown that include soy proteins in one's diet on a regular basis in the form of foods like tofu and tempeh may help reduce the course of kidney disease. As part of the renal diet, there are three minerals in particular that should be avoided. If the kidneys are damaged or diseased, the risk of dangerously high concentrations of these minerals in the blood increases. The kidneys are responsible for maintaining a healthy level of these minerals in the blood, but if they are damaged or diseased, the blood can build up dangerously high concentrations of these minerals. In this post, we will explore the risks associated with ingesting an excessive amount of phosphorus, potassium, and salt, as well as the foods that have to be avoided in order to do this.

On the other hand, you should keep away but also from any diet that has a significant amount of salt in its ingredients. Because sodium has the propensity to cause an increase in blood pressure, it is harmful to both the kidneys and the cardiovascular system. The additional strain placed on the kidneys as a result of having to filter more fluid at a faster pace owing to high blood pressure ultimately results in infection and the loss of renal function. High blood pressure and renal disease are two conditions that often occur together. Consuming meals that will cause a significant increase in our blood pressure is not a good idea if it is already elevated. This requires you to use less salt in your cooking and abstain from high-sodium convenience meals such as those served in fast food restaurants and restaurants that deliver food. Fortuitously, a large number of customers are unaware that some meals include unseen quantities of salt. All of these types of food are included in the coverage, including deli meats, canned and frozen meals, energy drinks, flavored and processed snacks.

In addition to sodium, potassium is another mineral that is present in a significant number of everyday meals. In spite of the fact that potassium is an essential component, the blood levels of this mineral must be carefully managed in order to guarantee the efficient functioning of these systems. It is possible for renal damage to cause an elevation in blood potassium levels, which may throw off fluid balance, raise the risk of cardiovascular disease, and cause other complications. As a result, the renal diet recommends cutting down on the amount of potassium that is consumed. The severity will be determined based on the results of the tests. Tomatoes, potatoes, bananas, almonds, seeds, pumpkin, and chocolate are all good examples of foods that are rich in potassium. In situations when there is an excessive amount of potassium, it may be essential to carry out a process that removes potassium from plants. This is due to the fact that it is impossible to entirely remove potassium from the environment.

Phosphorus is a mineral that should be consumed in moderation as part of a renal diet. This is an essential fact to keep in mind. Phosphorus may be found in substantial quantities in foods such as dairy products, meat and grains (including wheat), peanuts and legumes (including chocolate), coconut (including coconut milk), eggs, and beer. Phosphorus can also be found in beer. If blood phosphorus levels are high, it is imperative that careful attention be paid to the phosphorus content of ordinarily healthy foods such as eggs and lentils. Phosphorus' participation in calcium control, which is critical for the development of healthy bones and teeth, is one of the mineral's most significant roles. Calcium management is needed for healthy bone and tooth production. Phosphorus may have an effect not only on the levels of sodium and potassium, but also on calcium and magnesium. A high amount of phosphorus in the blood, which prevents the body from absorbing calcium and is linked to kidney impairment, may put a person at risk for developing osteoporosis. As we have seen, kidney damage may be caused by high blood pressure, and taking an excessive amount of phosphorus may be a factor in the development of this illness. One further recommendation for the greatest diet for renal health is to have a diet that is mostly alkaline. When a person has renal illness, it is more difficult for their kidneys to carry out their job, which is to maintain a constant pH in the blood. Eliminating acidic foods and drinks from the diet is thus very beneficial and will contribute to a more expedited recuperation of the kidneys. Within the context of this renal diet, the question of whether or not to include protein is one that receives a lot of attention. Because of this, the answer to this question is contingent, in part, on the state of your kidneys.

The amount of salt, potassium, phosphorus, calcium, albumin, and urea that are already present in your blood influences the number of nutrients that you are able to absorb from meals. These values are measured immediately before and after a dialysis session. The patient's urine output and weight gain are taken into consideration to determine the appropriate level of fluid restriction between dialysis treatments. It is imperative that any liquid that is lost by perspiration, urination, or any other means be replaced with water. Keeping close track of your weight on a consistent basis is an excellent habit to get into if you want to detect fluid retention, which may be an early sign of renal impairment. Keeping renal function at a healthy level may buy some time before it is essential to begin dialysis. It is essential to take care of the patient's health in general, which includes preventing the advancement of their illness, maintaining a stable blood pressure level, and reducing the patient's protein consumption as well as their catabolism. The findings of the patient's blood chemistry tests will help the physician determine whether or not to suggest making any minor alterations to the patient's low protein renal diet. a. In some people, delaying the onset of renal failure can be accomplished by keeping their daily protein consumption at or below 50 grammes, which has been shown to have a high physiologic value; however, there is a substantial amount of debate regarding whether or not to restrict protein consumption and how to do so. Both the health of your kidneys and the quantity of protein that your body requires to perform at its best are important considerations when determining how much protein you are able to consume. When proteins are broken down, byproducts are produced. These byproducts are then flushed out of the body via the circulatory system.

One waste product that fulfils this criterion is urea, which is an example of the trash. Urea may be flushed out of a body that is functioning normally thanks to the kidneys. People who have renal illness should nonetheless consume protein for their own health, despite the fact that this is not the best situation. When a client's illness becomes worse, they lose the capacity and drive to maintain a healthy diet for themselves. It might be difficult to consume sufficient calories from sources other than protein while still meeting one's daily protein needs. In order to meet the body's nutritional requirements, it may be required to consume elemental diets, enteral feedings, or complete parenteral nutrition in addition to, or even in instead of, the typical amount of food that one consumes on a daily basis.

Chapter 2: 5 Elements to Monitor in The Renal Diet and Their Role in The Body

Alterations to one's food and nutrition may help improve one's ability to regulate the sickness and may even cause it to progress more slowly. Taking care of main risk factors for kidney failure, such as diabetes and high blood pressure, is essential not just for avoiding future problems but also for extending survival time.

When it comes to consuming a diet that is healthy for your kidneys, there are some nutrients that are more vital than others. Make an appointment with a nutritionist so that you may create a meal plan that is personalized to your particular needs.

The following dietary limitations are required for patients who have chronic renal disease:

Protein

It is of the utmost importance to keep up a healthy protein consumption. Considerations such as height and overall health are taken into account. Protein is necessary for the proper functioning of the immune system, the healing of wounds, and the production of enzymes and hormones. Because damaged kidneys are less efficient at cleaning out waste products, it is imperative that dietary protein consumption be reduced in order to avoid the build-up of potentially harmful substances. Maintain portions of meat that are about equivalent in size to a typical deck of playing cards.

Sodium

The increased stress on the heart and lungs that results from sodium's impact on fluid retention and blood pressure is one of those consequences. There is a widespread misunderstanding that if you do not add salt to your meal, you will consume an appropriate quantity of sodium. However, the foods that we buy, such as cereals, meat, soups, sandwiches, and meals from restaurants, already account for more than 70% of the daily salt consumption of the average American. A consumption of 1,500 to 2,000 milligrams of salt per day is possible while adhering to a low-sodium diet.

Potassium

The mineral potassium may be found in a wide variety of foods. Because potassium is essential for proper muscle function, consuming excessive amounts of the mineral might have adverse effects. When kidney function deteriorates, the body's natural capacity to manage the concentration of different minerals in the blood becomes impaired, which may lead to serious health complications. As a consequence of this, there is a possibility that potassium and phosphorus may build up in the blood. A lack of potassium or an excess of potassium both have the potential to interfere with the normal function of your muscles. Potatoes, tomatoes, melons, oranges, orange juice, bananas, dairy products, and salt substitutes such as Morton Lite Salt and No Salt are examples of foods and liquids that are high in potassium content. If you have high blood potassium, you should limit your consumption of certain foods or completely avoid them.

Phosphorus

When both of your kidneys are working as they should, the amounts of phosphorus in your body will be consistent. Hyperphosphatemia develops when the levels of phosphorus in the blood are elevated and the kidneys are unable to adequately filter waste products. Phosphorus may be found in a variety of foods, but the ones that contain the most of it include ready-to-eat meals, processed cheese, packaged goods, and some drinks. Phosphoric acid, calcium phosphate, and hexametaphosphate are some of the substances that spring to mind while thinking of hypothetical instances. Because of the naturally occurring phosphorus in dairy products, almonds, and whole grains, it is possible that you may need to restrict the amount of these foods you consume.

Calcium

Calcium homeostasis is also thrown off by kidney failure. While consuming the recommended amount of calcium every day is essential for maintaining strong bones, exceeding that amount may cause calcium to accumulate in the blood vessels of the body. If you already have high amounts of calcium in your blood, you shouldn't consume foods or drinks that have been fortified with calcium. In addition, if you are using calcium supplements, you should make your doctor aware of this fact. Maintaining a diet that is healthy for the kidneys may seem to be a significant amount of additional labour and restriction. By limiting or eliminating certain foods from the diet, it may be possible to stop the accumulation of waste products in the blood, boost kidney function, and protect the body from suffering more harm in the future. It is highly suggested that you consult with a qualified dietitian in order to develop a diet that is safe for your kidneys and that is adapted to meet your specific needs.

Fluids

Those who are on a dialysis fluid restriction diet are advised to limit the amount of fluid they eat each day to no more than 32 ounces. Your doctor or dietitian will go through your specific requirements for fluid intake in great detail. By keeping a journal of everything you eat and drink throughout the day, you can easily keep track of the quantity of liquids that you take in on a daily basis. It might be beneficial to plan out what you will drink and when you will drink it during the day. If, for example, you have an important function scheduled for the evening, you should limit the number of fluids that you consume during the day.

There is a possibility that over time, you may progressively generate less urine on a daily basis. At a minimum of once every three months, you should maintain a record of the amount of urine you produce. This will allow your physician and nutritionist to determine whether or not you need any dietary adjustments. Some people choose to collect their urine in a throwaway cup of 20 fluid ounces when they do so. Before you begin cooking, make marks at half-cup intervals on your measuring cup or container. Urine should be saved for a full day before being measured and recorded so that the results may be discussed with both your primary care physician and your dietitian.

When beginning dialysis, it is usual to be told to reduce the amount of fluid that you consume. This is especially true if dialysis is being performed three times per week and urine production is decreasing. Most of the time, patients undergoing in-home hemodialysis get no fluids other than the minimal minimum required to clean their tubes. The accumulation of fluid may make it harder to breathe, which can lead to deem and high blood pressure. The state of the patient is what determines how much fluid can be removed during dialysis while still being safe. Some of the unpleasant consequences of exceeding fluid restrictions and having to remove excess water include cramping in the muscles, low blood pressure that can lead to nausea, weakness, and dizziness, and the possibility of having to undergo additional dialysis treatments in order to remove the fluid.

Chapter 3: Breakfast Recipes

A Blend of Apples and Chai

Preparation Time: 30 Minutes
Servings: 2

Nutritional Analysis:
Total Calories: 219
Total fat: 12g
Protein: 9g
Carbohydrates: 21g

Ingredients:

- 1.5 oz of sweetened rice milk
- 1 bag of chai tea
- 1 apple, prepared by peeling, coring, and dicing
- 2 cups of crushed ice

Instructions:

- Warm the rice milk in a medium saucepan over low heat for 5 minutes, or until steaming.
- Turn off the heat and let the milk soak with the tea bag.
- Tea bags and milk should be left in the fridge for around 30 minutes.
- Take out the tea bag and gently squeeze it to extract the flavor.
- The apple, milk, and ice should be blended until smooth.
- Serve immediately in two glasses.

Fruity Holiday Parfait

Preparation Time: 20 Minutes
Servings: 1

Nutritional Analysis:
Total Calories: 200
Total fat: 18g
Protein: 14g
Carbohydrates: 33g

Ingredients:

- 1 cup of vanilla-flavored rice milk, room temperature
- 1/2 tbsp room temperature cream cheese, plain
- 1 tbsp granulated sugar
- 1/2 tsp. of cinnamon powder
- 1 cup of broken up Meringues (here)
- 2 cups of fresh blueberries
- Suggested Ingredients: 1 cup of fresh strawberries, sliced

Instructions:

- Mix the milk, cream cheese, sugar, and cinnamon in a small bowl.
- Put a quarter cup of the crumbled biscuit into the bottom of each of four (6-ounce) cups.
- Top the cookies with a quarter cup of the cream cheese filling.
- Sprinkle a quarter cup of the berries over the cream cheese.
- Cookies, cream cheese mixture, and berries are layered in each cup.
- Put in the fridge for an hour, then serve cold.

Breakfast Hot Cereal with a Variety of Grains

Preparation Time: 20 Minutes
Servings: 1

Nutritional Analysis:
Total Calories: 279
Total fat: 10g
Protein: 7g
Carbohydrates: 14g

Ingredients:

- 2 glasses of water
- 2 cups of vanilla rice milk
- 6 tbsp bulgur, raw
- 2 tbsp of raw, whole buckwheat
- 1 cup of apple, peeled and sliced
- 6 tbsp of unseasoned couscous
- 1/2 tsp of cinnamon powder

Instructions:

- The water and milk should be heated in a medium saucepan over medium heat.
- Cook until the liquid has reduced by half, then stir in the bulgur, buckwheat, and apple.
- Turn the heat down to low and simmer for 20-25 minutes, stirring regularly, or until the bulgur is cooked.
- Turn off the heat and mix in the couscous and cinnamon before returning the pan to the stove.
- Cover the pot and let the cereal sit for 10 minutes at room temperature before serving.

Creme de Maze

Preparation Time: 28 Minutes
Servings: 3

Nutritional Analysis:
Total Calories: 200
Total fat: 8g
Protein: 15g
Carbohydrates: 20g

Ingredients:
- Grease a baking dish with unsalted butter.
- 2 tbsp of all-purpose flour
- 2 tsp of the baking soda alternative Ener-G
- 3 eggs
- 34 cups of room temperature rice milk, unsweetened
- Unsalted butter, melted (about 3 tablespoons)
- 2 tbsp of light sour cream
- 2 tbsp of white sugar
- 2 cups of thawed corn kernels

Instructions:
- Get the oven up to temperature, preferably 350 °F.
- Butter a square baking dish that's 8 inches by 8 inches and put it aside.
- Mix the flour and the baking soda replacement in a small bowl, and put it aside.
- Combine the eggs, rice milk, butter, sour cream, and sugar in a medium bowl and whisk until smooth.
- Mix the flour and baking powder into the eggs until the mixture is uniform.
- Cooked corn should be added to the batter and well combined.
- Sprinkle the batter over the vegetables and bake for 40 minutes, or until
- The proof is already in the pudding.
- Wait 15 minutes before serving the pudding warm.

Bread Pudding with Rhubarb

Preparation Time: 30 Minutes
Servings: 2

Nutritional Analysis:
Total Calories: 252
Total fat: 9g
Protein: 10g
Carbohydrates: 36g

Ingredients:

- Grease a baking dish with unsalted butter.
- 1 ½ cups of plain rice milk
- 3 eggs
- ½ cup of white sugar, granulated
- 1 tbsp of cornstarch
- 34 of a vanilla bean
- 10 slices of white bread, each one inch in thickness.
- 2 cups of diced fresh rhubarb

Instructions:

- Get the oven up to temperature, preferably 350 °F.
- Butter a square baking dish that's 8 inches by 8 inches and put it aside.
- Mix the rice milk, eggs, sugar, and cornstarch in a large bowl.
- Put the vanilla bean scrapings and milk in a bowl and stir together.
- Toss the cubed bread into the egg mixture and toss until it is well coated.
- Stir in the rhubarb chunks.
- In a large bowl, combine the bread and eggs and let aside for 30 minutes.
- Put the ingredients in the dish you've prepared, cover it with foil, and bake for 40 minutes.
- Remove the lid and bake the bread pudding for a further 10 minutes, or until it has reached the desired color and firmness.
- Serve hot.

Muffins Flavored with Cinnamon and Nutmeg Studded with Blueberries.

Preparation Time: 35 Minutes
Servings: 1

Nutritional Analysis:
Total Calories: 250
Total fat: 16g
Protein: 16g
Carbohydrates: 28g

Ingredients:

- 2 cups of unsweetened rice milk
- 1 tbsp of apple cider vinegar
- 70 oz of all-purpose flour
- Sugar, Granulated, 1 Cup
- 1 tbsp of substitute of baking soda
- 1tbsp of ground cinnamon
- ½ tsp of nutmeg powder
- 1 tsp of ginger powder
- ½ cup of canola oil
- 2 tsp of pure vanilla extract
- ½ cup of fresh blueberries

Instructions:

- Get the oven up to temperature, preferably 375 °F.
- Get out a muffin tin and line the cups with paper liners.
- Rice milk and vinegar may be combined in a small dish and let to sit for 10 minutes.
- Sift the flour, sugar, baking powder, and baking soda replacement into a large basin, then whisk in the butter.
- Combine the spices (cinnamon, nutmeg, and ginger) until uniform. To the milk and oil, add the vanilla extract and whisk until smooth.
- To the dry ingredients, add the milk mixture and whisk until incorporated.
- Combine the blueberries into the mixture. Make sure the muffin cups are full before you start spooning in the batter.
- Put the muffins in the oven for 25 to 30 minutes, or until they are brown and a toothpick comes out clean.
- A clean knife blade when put into the middle of a muffin.
- The muffins need at least 15 minutes to cool before being served.

Snack Wrap with Fruit and Cheese for the Morning Meal

Preparation Time: 15 Minutes
Servings: 2

Nutritional Analysis:
Total Calories: 279
Total fat: 11g
Protein: 10g
Carbohydrates: 38g

Ingredients:

- 2 corn or flour tortillas, each measuring about 6 inches in diameter
- 2 tsp of cream cheese, plain
- 1 apple, peel, core, and thinly slice
- 1 tbsp of honey

Instructions:

- Spread 1 tablespoon of cream cheese over each tortilla, leaving a half-inch border around the borders.
- Place apple slices on cream cheese, just off the center of the tortilla on the side nearest to you, leaving approximately two inches on each side and 2 inches on the bottom.
- Add a little of honey to the apples.
- The tortillas should be folded in half lengthwise, with the edge laid over the apples.
- The closest edge of the tortilla should be folded over the fruit and the side.
- Tightly wrap the tortilla by rolling it away from you. Use another tortilla and do it all over again.

Egg-In-The-Hole

Preparation Time: 10 Minutes
Servings: 3

Nutritional Analysis:
Total Calories: 190
Total fat: 9g
Protein: 6g
Carbohydrates: 40g

Ingredients:

- 2 slices of Italian bread, each about 2 an inch thick.
- ¼ of butter, unsalted
- 2 eggs
- 2 tsp of finely chopped fresh chives

Instructions:

- Shake in some chili pepper
- Cracked black pepper, just ground
- Remove a 2-inch diameter circle from the middle of each slice of bread using a cookie cutter or a tiny glass.
- The butter is melted over medium heat in a large, nonstick pan.
- After toasting the bread for a minute on one side, turn it over and continue to cook it for another minute.
- Cook for 2 minutes, or until the eggs are set and the bread is golden brown after cracking them into the holes.
- Finish with some chopped chives, cayenne, and black pepper.
- Add two more minutes to the cooking time of the bread.
- Place an egg in the center of a hole in each dish. Serve immediately.

Delicious Pancakes

Preparation Time: 30 Minutes
Servings: 1

Nutritional Analysis:
Total Calories: 219
Total fat: 10g
Protein: 8g
Carbohydrates: 21g

Ingredients:

- 2 eggs
- ½ cup of rice milk, unsweetened
- 14 cups of all-purpose flour
- ¼ tsp of cinnamon powder
- Crush nutmeg and measure out a pinch
- Pan release spray, for use in the kitchen

Instructions:

- Turn the oven temperature up to 450 °F.
- Eggs and rice milk should be mixed together in a medium bowl.
- Do not overmix after adding the flour, cinnamon, and nutmeg; stir until just combined.
- Pre-heat the oven to 450 °F and coat a 9-inch ovenproof pan with cooking spray.
- Carefully lift the pan and add the pancake batter.
- Place the pan back in the oven and bake the pancake for 20 minutes, or until it reaches the desired doneness.
- Until the edges are crispy and it has puffed up.
- In order to serve, slice the pancake in half.

French Toast Stuffed with Strawberries and Cream Cheese

Preparation Time: 18 Minutes
Servings: 2

Nutritional Analysis:
Total Calories: 249
Total fat: 8g
Protein: 9g
Carbohydrates: 30g

Ingredients:
- Spray oil for cooking, to coat the baking dish
- ½ a jar of regular cream cheese
- 4 tsp of strawberry preserves
- Thick white bread cut into 8 pieces
- 2 beaten eggs
- ½ cup of rice milk, unsweetened
- 1 tsp of vanilla extract
- 1 tbsp of granulated sugar
- ¼ tsp of cinnamon powder

Instructions:
- Get the oven up to temperature, preferably 350 °F.
- Prepare a baking dish, 8 inches by 8 inches, by spraying it with cooking spray and setting it aside.
- Cream cheese and jam may be combined in a small dish with a good whisk.
- On 4 pieces of bread, spread 3 tablespoons of the cream cheese mixture.
- In between two of the remaining four slices.
- Whisk the eggs, milk, and vanilla together in a medium bowl.
- To prepare, just soak the sandwiches in the egg wash and then arrange them on a baking dish.

Chapter 4: Soups and Salads Recipes

Soup with Ground Beef and Rice

Preparation Time: 30 Minutes
Servings: 1

Nutritional Analysis:
Total Calories: 269
Total fat: 10g
Protein: 8g
Carbohydrates: 30g

Ingredients:

- ½ pound of lean beef
- ½ of a tiny, chopped sweet onion
- 1 tsp of chopped garlic
- 2.5 ounces of liquid
- Beef broth, low in salt, produced at home, 1 cup
- 1 ½ cups of raw long-grain white rice
- 1 sliced celery stalk
- Cut 1 pound of fresh green beans into 1-inch pieces (about 1/2 cup).
- 1 tsp of fresh thyme
- Cracked black pepper, just ground

Instructions:

- Put the ground beef in a large saucepan and set it over medium heat.
- For approximately 6 minutes, while tossing often, brown the meat well in a sauté pan.
- Remove the fatty residue from the pan and add the onion and garlic.
- For approximately 3 minutes, or until softened, sauté the veggies.
- To the rice and celery, add the water and beef broth.
- Once the soup has come to a boil, lower the heat and let it simmer for about 30 minutes, or until the rice is done.
- Green beans and thyme should be added and cooked for three minutes at a low simmer.
- Turn off the heat and season the soup with pepper. Serve immediately.

Soup with Bulgur and Turkey

Preparation Time: 30 Minutes
Servings: 1

Nutritional Analysis:
Total Calories: 271
Total fat: 10g
Protein: 8g
Carbohydrates: 36g

Ingredients:

- 1 tsp of olive oil
- ½ pound of ground turkey, 93% lean and cooked
- 2 medium-sized sweet onion, diced
- 1 tsp of chopped garlic
- 4 cups of water
- 1 cup of chicken broth
- 1 sliced celery stalk
- 1 carrot, thinly sliced
- ¼ cup of finely sliced red onion
- 2 tbsp of bulgur
- 2 stale bay leaves
- 2 tsp of chopped fresh parsley
- 1 tsp of fresh chopped sage
- 1 tsp of fresh thyme
- Tease out some crushed red pepper

Instructions:

- Cracked black pepper, just ground
- Put the olive oil in a big pot and set it over medium heat. Turkey should be sautéed for approximately 5 minutes, or until done.
- To soften the onions and garlic, add them to the pan and cook for approximately 3 minutes. Place the bay leaves, celery, carrot, cabbage, bulgur, and chicken stock into a large pot.
- When the soup has come to a boil, decrease the heat to low and let it simmer for approximately 35 minutes, or until the bulgur and veggies are soft.
- Get rid of the bay leaves and mix in the fresh herbs and spices like parsley, sage, thyme, and red pepper flakes.
- Add pepper and it will taste great.

Salad with Waldorf Dressing and Turkey

Preparation Time: 40 Minutes
Servings: 3

Nutritional Analysis:
Total Calories: 245
Total fat: 12g
Protein: 18g
Carbohydrates: 35g

Ingredients:
- 2 oz unseasoned turkey breast
- 3 medium-sized of red apples
- 1 cup of celery
- 2 cups of chopped onion
- 1 tbsp of mayonnaise
- 6 cups of apple juice

Instructions:
- Cube the turkey, apple, and celery, and cut the onion very finely.
- Mix the turkey, apple, celery, and onion in a medium bowl.
- Stir in the mayonnaise and apple juice until everything is evenly combined.
- Put in the fridge and wait to serve.

Balsamic Vinaigrette-Dressed Lettuce and Carrot Salad

Preparation Time: 30 Minutes
Servings: 1

Nutritional Analysis:
Total Calories: 219
Total fat: 10g
Protein: 16g
Carbohydrates: 38g

Ingredients:
- 1 ½ cups of olive oil
- 4 tbsp of balsamic vinegar
- 2 tbsp of fresh oregano, finely chopped
- Tease out some crushed red pepper
- Cracked black pepper, just ground
- 4 ¼ cups of shredded green leaf lettuce
- 1 shredded carrot
- ¾ cup fresh green beans, cut into 1-inch pieces
- 3 large thinly sliced radishes

Instructions:
- Mix the olive oil, balsamic vinegar, oregano, and salt in a small basin.
- Add crushed red pepper.
- Put some pepper on it.
- Mix the lettuce, carrot, green beans, and radishes in a big bowl.
- Soak the veggies in the vinaigrette and mix to coat.
- Salad should be served on four dishes.

Strawberry Watercress Salad with Almond Dressing

Preparation Time: 40 Minutes
Servings: 2

Nutritional Analysis:
Total Calories: 229
Total fat: 15g
Protein: 16g
Carbohydrates: 21g

Ingredients:

- ¼ mug of olive oil
- ¼ mug of rice vinegar
- 1 tbsp of honey
- ½ tsp of natural almond flavor
- ¼ tsp of mustard seed
- Cracked black pepper, just ground
- 2 cups of watercress, coarsely chopped
- Green leaf lettuce, to the volume of two cups
- ½ of a red onion, thinly sliced
- 1 ½ cups of chopped English cucumber
- Strawberries, around a cup's worth
- Stir the olive oil and rice vinegar together in a small basin until
- Emulsified.
- Honey, almond essence, mustard, and pepper should be whisked together and placed aside.

Instructions:

- Mix the watercress, green leaf lettuce, onion, cucumber, and strawberries in a big bowl.
- Incorporate the dressing into the salad by pouring it on top.

Salsa with Limón

Preparation Time: 20 Minutes
Servings: 3

Nutritional Analysis:
Total Calories: 219
Total fat: 6g
Protein: 16g
Carbohydrates: 30g

Ingredients:
- 1/3 cup of light cream
- ¼ cup of lemon juice, squeezed
- 2 tbsp of white sugar
- 1 tsp of finely chopped fresh dill
- 2 tsp of finely sliced scallion (just the greens, please)
- A pinch of freshly ground black pepper
- A cucumber from England, thinly sliced
- 1 ½ cups of shredded red cabbage

Instructions:
- Mix the cream, lemon juice, sugar, dill, scallion, and salt, pepper, and other seasonings until everything is combined.
- Cucumber and cabbage should be mixed together in a big basin.
- Make sure to refrigerate the salad for at least an hour before serving.
- Make sure to give it a good stir before serving.

Salad with Asparagus and Leaf Lettuce with Raspberries

Preparation Time: 20 Minutes
Servings: 2

Nutritional Analysis:
Total Calories: 276
Total fat: 13g
Protein: 17g
Carbohydrates: 21g

Ingredients

- Green leaf lettuce, to the volume of two cups
- 1 cup of peeled, long-noodle-shaped asparagus
- 1 scallion, both green and white sections, sliced
- 1 cup raspberries
- 2 tbsp of balsamic vinegar
- Cracked black pepper, just ground

Instructions:

- Arrange the lettuce equally on 4 serving plates.
- Make a pretty arrangement with the asparagus and scallion on top of the leaves.
- Spread the raspberries out in an equal layer over the salads.
- The salads would benefit from a little application of balsamic vinegar.
- Put some pepper on it.

Salad Waldorf

Preparation Time: 30 Minutes
Servings: 2

Nutritional Analysis:
Total Calories: 262
Total fat: 9g
Protein: 8g
Carbohydrates: 30g

Ingredients:
- 3 cups of torn green leaf lettuce
- 1 cup of grapes, halved
- 3 stalks of chopped celery
- 1 large apple, core, peel and coarsely chop
- ½ cup of light sour cream
- 2 tsp of lemon juice, freshly squeezed
- 1 tbsp of granulated sugar
- Place a bed of lettuce on each of four plates.

Instructions:
- Mix the grapes, celery, and apple in a little bowl.
- Blend the sour cream, lemon juice, and sugar in a separate small bowl.
- Combine the sour cream and grapes and whisk to combine.
- Place an equal amount of the dressed grape mixture on each dish.

Salad with Ginger Beef

Preparation Time: 40 Minutes
Servings: 3

Nutritional Analysis:
Total Calories: 226
Total fat: 18g
Protein: 9g
Carbohydrates: 31g

Ingredients:

- 2 tbsp of olive oil
- 2 tbsp of lime juice, preferably freshly squeezed
- 1 tbsp of grated fresh ginger
- 2 tbsp of minced garlic equaling
- ½ pound of flank steak
- ¼ mug of olive oil
- ¼ mug of rice vinegar
- 1 lime's juice
- 1 lime's worth of zest
- 1 tbsp of honey
- 1 tsp of fresh thyme
- 4 cups of torn green leaf lettuce
- ½ red onion, thinly sliced
- ½ oz of sliced radishes

Instructions:

- Blend the olive oil, lime juice, ginger, and garlic together in a small bowl.
- After adding the flank steak to the marinade, make sure all sides are coated.
- Marinate in the fridge for one hour, covered with plastic wrap.
- Toss the marinade while removing the meat.
- Grill the steak to desired doneness (approximately 5 minutes each side, depending on the thickness) over medium heat, rotating once.
- Take the steak out, set it on a cutting board, and let it rest for ten minutes.
- Cutting thin slices against the grain of the meat.
- Olive oil, rice vinegar, lime juice, lime zest, and salt should be mixed together in a small basin.
- Combine the honey and thyme and put them aside.
- Prepare 6 salads by dividing the lettuce, onion, and radishes among them.
- The vinaigrette should be poured over each salad individually.
- Sprinkle the sliced meat on top of each salad.

Chapter 5: Poultry and Meat Recipes

Crostini With Roasted Red Peppers, Chicken, And Feta

Preparation Time: 20 Minutes
Servings: 1

Nutritional Analysis:
Total Calories: 219
Total fat:6g
Protein: 8g
Carbohydrates: 35g

Ingredients:

- 2 tbsp of olive oil
- ½ tsp of chopped garlic
- 4 pieces of French bread
- Chopped roasted red bell pepper (1 pepper)
- 4 oz of shredded chicken breast
- ¼ tsp dried oregano

Instructions:

- Turn the oven temperature up to 400 °F.
- Prepare an aluminum foil-lined baking sheet.
- Put the olive oil and garlic in a little bowl and stir to combine.
- Spread the olive oil mixture on both sides of the bread slices.
- Toast the bread in a preheated oven for till golden, rotating once.
- Five minutes, or until both sides are crisp and brown.
- Combine the red pepper, chicken, and basil in a medium bowl and mix well.
- Serve the roasted red pepper mixture on top of each piece of toasted bread.

Skewers with Chicken and Veggies

Preparation Time: 20 Minutes
Servings: 1

Nutritional Analysis:
Total Calories: 229
Total fat: 12g
Protein: 16g
Carbohydrates: 36g

Ingredients:

- 2 tbsp of olive oil
- 2 tsp of lemon juice, freshly squeezed
- ½ tsp of chopped garlic
- 1 tbsp of fresh thyme, chopped
- 8 pieces of 4-ounce boneless, skinless chicken breast
- An eight-piece serving of 1 tiny summer squash
- 1 ½ of a medium onion, sliced into 8 pieces
- Olive oil, lemon juice, garlic, and thyme are combined in a medium bowl.

Instructions:

- Mix in the chicken and coat well.
- Marinating the chicken in the fridge for an hour is recommended. Cover the bowl with plastic wrap and refrigerate.
- Skewer the chicken, onion, and squash cubes onto four big skewers, spreading the chicken and veggies equally.
- In a grill pan or on a barbeque set to medium heat, cook the skewers, flipping at least twice, for 10 to 2 minutes, or until the chicken is fully cooked.

Lettuce Wraps with Five Spice Chicken

Preparation Time: 30 Minutes
Servings: 1

Nutritional Analysis:
Total Calories: 218
Total fat: 19g
Protein: 12g
Carbohydrates: 40g

Ingredients:
- 6 oz of chopped, cooked chicken breast
- 1 scallion, chopped
- ½ red apple, peeled and diced
- 2 cups of mung bean sprouts
- 1 ¼ cups of coarsely chopped English cucumber
- 1 lime's juice
- 1 lime's worth of zest
- 2 tsp of finely chopped fresh coriander
- ½ tsp of Chinese Five Spice Powder
- A head of Boston lettuce with 8 leaves

Instructions:
- Chicken, scallions, apple, bean sprouts, cucumber, lime juice, lime zest, cilantro, and five-spice powder should all be combined in a big dish.
- Divide the chicken filling amongst the 8 lettuce leaves.
- The chicken filling may be wrapped in lettuce leaves and served.

Herb and Lemon Chicken

Preparation Time: 30 Minutes
Servings: 1

Nutritional Analysis:
Total Calories: 219
Total fat: 6g
Protein: 16g
Carbohydrates: 45g

Ingredients:

- 2 ounces of boneless, skinless chicken breast, sliced into 8 strips
- 1 egg white
- 2 tbsp of water, split
- ½ cup of bread crumbs
- ¼ cup of unsalted butter, split
- 1 lemon's juice
- 1 lemon gratings
- 1 tbsp of finely chopped fresh basil
- 1 tsp of chopped fresh thyme
- To decorate, use lemon slices.

Instructions:

- Flatten the chicken strips by placing them between two pieces of plastic wrap and pounding them with a mallet or rolling pin.
- The egg and 1 tablespoon of water should be mixed together in a medium bowl.
- To a separate medium bowl, add the bread crumbs.
- Chicken strips should be dredged in egg, then bread crumbs, and finally placed on a platter.
- Two tablespoons of the butter should be melted in a large pan over medium heat.
- To ensure that the strips are well cooked and become golden, sauté them in the butter for approximately 3 minutes, stirring once.
- Put the chicken on a serving dish.
- Stir in the remaining 1 tablespoon of water along with the lemon juice, lemon zest, basil, and thyme until the mixture simmers.
- Turn off the heat and whisk in the extra 2 tablespoons of butter to the sauce.
- The chicken should be served with the lemon sauce poured over it and some lemon wedges for garnish.

Satay Chicken from Asia

Preparation Time: 30 Minutes
Servings: 3

Nutritional Analysis:
Total Calories: 259
Total fat: 10g
Protein: 16g
Carbohydrates: 45g

Ingredients:
- 2 fresh squeezed limes
- 2 tbsp of dark sugar
- 1 tbsp of minced garlic
- 2 tbsp of cumin seeds, ground
- Skinless, boneless chicken breasts (2 ounces) sliced into 2 strips

Instructions:
- Combine the lime juice, brown sugar, garlic, and cumin in a large bowl and mix well.
- Marinate the chicken strips for an hour in the fridge after adding them to the dish.
- Prepare a medium-high flame in the grill.
- Take the chicken out of the marinade and skewer it onto a wooden skewer that has been dipped in water.
- Cook the chicken on the grill for approximately 4 minutes each side, or until it is no longer pink in the center.

Curry Chicken

Preparation Time: 30 Minutes
Servings: 2

Nutritional Analysis:
Total Calories: 279
Total fat: 11g
Protein: 14g
Carbohydrates: 35g

Ingredients:

- 1 ½ tbsp of pineapple juice
- 1 tbsp of balsamic vinegar
- 1 tsp of fresh ginger, grated
- 1 tsp of chopped garlic
- 2 tbsp of cornstarch
- 2 tbsp of olive oil
- Chicken breast (boneless, skinless, 2 oz., diced 1 in.)
- ¼ cup broccoli florets
- ½ cup of carrots, sliced thinly
- 2 cups of fresh green beans
- 3 cups of white rice

Instructions:

- Stir the balsamic vinegar, garlic, ginger, and cornstarch together in a small bowl and put aside.
- Heat the olive oil in a large pan or wok set over medium heat.
- For approximately 6 minutes, or until the chicken is done in the center, sauté it.
- Take the finished chicken and place it on a serving dish.
- Stir-fry the cauliflower, carrots, and green beans for 4 minutes, or until the veggies are crisp and tender, depending on their firmness.
- When the chicken is done, put it back in the pan and toss it to mix with the sauce.
- It's time to add the sauce, so move the chicken and veggies to one side of the pan.
- Incorporate thickening ingredients and cook, stirring constantly, for 2 minutes.
- Return the chicken and veggies to the sauce and stir to coat.
- The rice is for dipping.

Low Potassium Spiced Chicken with Olive Oil

Preparation Time: 25 Minutes
Servings: 1

Nutritional Analysis:
Total Calories: 249
Total fat: 10g
Protein: 16g
Carbohydrates: 46g

Ingredients:

- 3 tbsp of olive oil, separated
- 6 chicken thighs, skinned and boneless
- 1-inch mild onion
- 2 tbsp of minced garlic equaling
- 1 tsp of fresh ginger, grated
- 1 tbsp of spicy curry seasoning
- ¼ mug water
- ¼ cup coconut milk
- 2 tsp of finely chopped fresh coriander

Instructions:

- Two tablespoons of the oil should be heated in a large pan over medium heat.
- After approximately 10 minutes, or when the thighs are no longer pink in the center, add the chicken.
- Fully browned up.
- Using the tongs, transfer the chicken to a platter.
- After adding the remaining tablespoon of oil to the pan, sauté the onion, garlic, and ginger for 3 minutes, or until they are softened to your liking.
- Curry, water, and coconut milk should be combined and stirred in.
- Put the chicken back in the pan and bring the broth to a boil.
- Simmer for 25 minutes with the lid on, or until the chicken is fork-tender and the sauce has thickened.
- Cilantro goes well on top.

Low Sodium Spicy Chicken

Preparation Time: 30 Minutes
Servings: 3

Nutritional Analysis:
Total Calories: 289
Total fat: 16g
Protein: 26g
Carbohydrates: 38g

Ingredients:
- ½ of a tiny, chopped sweet onion
- ¼ cup of lemon juice, squeezed
- 1 tbsp of dried oregano
- 1 tsp of chopped garlic
- 1 tsp of paprika, sweet
- ½ tsp of ground cumin
- 1 ½ cup of olive oil
- 5 chicken thighs, skinned and boneless

Instructions:
- Blend or process the onion, lemon juice, oregano, garlic, paprika, and cumin.
- To combine the constituents, pulse the blender a few times.
- While the blender is running, slowly drizzle in the olive oil.
- Chicken thighs should be marinated in the marinade for at least an hour before being cooked.
- The bag should be sealed and placed in the fridge for 2 hours, during which time it should be turned twice.
- Take the thighs out of the marinade and throw away the leftover marinade.
- The grill should be preheated too medium.
- Cook the chicken on a grill for 20 minutes, flipping once, or until an instant-read thermometer registers 165 degrees Fahrenheit.

Pork Chops with Pesto

Preparation Time: 30 Minutes
Servings: 2

Nutritional Analysis:
Total Calories: 279
Total fat: 6g
Protein: 16g
Carbohydrates: 41g

Ingredients:

- 4 boneless, fat-trimmed pork top-loin chops (3 ounces each)
- 8 tbsp of herb pesto
- ½ cup of bread crumbs
- ½ tsp of olive oil

Instructions:

- Turn the oven temperature up to 450 °F.
- Preparation Steps: Line a baking sheet with foil and put aside.
- On both sides of each pork chop, spread one teaspoon of pesto.
- Coat each pork chop lightly with the bread crumbs.
- Warm the oil in a big pan over moderate heat.
- Cook the pork chops for approximately 5 minutes total, browning on both sides.
- Make room on the baking pan for the pork chops.
- The internal temperature of the pork has to reach 145 degrees Fahrenheit, so plan on baking it for around 10 minutes.

Succulent Pork Souvlaki

Preparation Time: 30 Minutes
Servings: 1

Nutritional Analysis:
Total Calories: 298
Total fat: 13g
Protein: 16g
Carbohydrates: 40g

Ingredients:
- 3 tbsp of olive oil
- 2 tsp of lemon juice
- 1 tsp of chopped garlic
- 1 tbsp of finely chopped fresh oregano
- A pinch of freshly ground black pepper
- Cubed 1-pound pork legs

Instructions:
- To make the dressing, combine the olive oil, lemon juice, garlic, oregano, and salt in a medium bowl and mix to combine.
- As well as pepper.
- Pork cubes should be added and tossed to coat.
- Marinate for 2 hours with the bowl covered and chilled in the fridge.
- Put the pig pieces on 8 skewers, either metal or wood, and then grill.
- Saturated with water.
- Turn the grill heat up to medium-high.
- Cooking time for the pork skewers on the grill should be around 2 minutes total, including flipping.
- In depth, but still delicious.

Pork Legs with Chili Rub

Preparation Time: 25 Minutes
Servings: 2

Nutritional Analysis:
Total Calories: 244
Total fat: 6g
Protein: 16g
Carbohydrates: 50g

Ingredients:
- 2 tbsp of chili powder.
- 2 tbsp of allspice, ground
- 1 ½ tbsp of ground cumin
- 1 tsp of garlic powder
- 1 tsp of ground cinnamon
- ½ tsp of freshly ground black pepper

Instructions:
- Shake in some chili pepper
- A pig leg roast without the bone that weighs one pound.
- 2-tablespoons of olive oil
- Allspice, cumin, chili powder, garlic powder, cinnamon, black pepper, and cayenne pepper should be combined in a small bowl.
- Coat the pig leg well with the spice rub.
- The pork loin should marinade for three hours in the fridge.
- Get the oven up to temperature, preferably 350 degrees Fahrenheit.
- Warm the olive oil in a large pan set over medium heat.
- After the pork loin has been seared on both sides, it should be baked.
- Keep the lid off and roast for 40 minutes, or until an instant-read thermometer registers 160 degrees Fahrenheit.
- After ten minutes in the oven, take the pork out and let it rest.
- Serve by slicing thinly.

Pan-Seared Beef Stir-Fry

Preparation Time: 30 Minutes
Servings: 2

Nutritional Analysis:
Total Calories: 295
Total fat: 13g
Protein: 18g
Carbohydrates: 39g

Ingredients:

- 1 lb of ground beef
- 2 cups of finely diced white onion
- ½ cup of cabbage, shredded
- ½ tsp herb pesto
- 6 bottom half of hamburger buns

Instructions:

- To cook the beef, sauté it with the onion in a large pan over medium heat for approximately 6 minutes.
- Sauté the cabbage for a further 3 minutes.
- After 1 minute, add the pesto and stir to heat through.
- Distribute the beef mixture into six servings, and place each on the bottom of a hamburger bun.

Meatloaf with a Sweet and Sour Sauce

Preparation Time: 20 Minutes
Servings: 1

Nutritional Analysis:
Total Calories: 219
Total fat: 10g
Protein: 16g
Carbohydrates: 46g

Ingredients:

- 1 lb ground beef, 95% lean
- ½ cup bread crumbs
- 2 cups of finely diced white onion
- 1 large egg
- 1 ½ tsp of dried oregano
- 1 tsp of fresh thyme
- 1 tsp of finely chopped fresh parsley
- A pinch of freshly ground black pepper
- 1 tbsp of dark sugar
- 1 tsp of vinegar
- ¼ tsp of dried garlic

Instructions:

- Get the oven up to temperature, preferably 350 °F.
- Combine the beef with the bread crumbs, onion, egg, basil, thyme, parsley, and pepper in a large mixing bowl.
- Pack the beef mixture into a loaf pan measuring 9 by 5.
- Mix the brown sugar, vinegar, and garlic powder in a separate small bowl.
- Liberally coat the meat with the brown sugar mixture.
- Cooking time for the beef loaf is around 50 minutes.
- After ten minutes, drain the meat loaf of any excess fat.

Steak With a Cool and Citrusy Salsa Made from Cucumbers and Cilantro on the Grill

Preparation Time: 30 Minutes
Servings: 2

Nutritional Analysis:
Total Calories: 29
Total fat: 17g
Protein: 6g
Carbohydrates:41g

Ingredients:

- 1 cup English cucumber, chopped
- ¼ cup of red bell pepper, cooked and diced
- 1 scallion, chopped green and white sections
- 2 tsp of finely chopped fresh coriander
- 1lime's juice
- 4 beef tenderloin steaks (about 3 ounces each)
- Olive oil

Instructions:

- Cracked black pepper, just ground
- Mix the bell pepper, scallion, cilantro, and lime juice with the cucumber in a medium bowl.
- Prepare a grill for medium heat.
- Remove the steaks from the fridge and set them out to warm up.
- Oil and pepper the steaks well.
- If you want your steaks medium-rare, grill them for around 5 minutes each side.
- If you can't find or don't want to use a grill, you can get perfectly cooked steaks by broiling them for 6 minutes on each side.
- Wait 10 minutes before serving the steaks.
- Salsa should be served with the steaks.

Traditional Pot Roast

Preparation Time: 30 Minutes
Servings: 2

Nutritional Analysis:
Total Calories: 279
Total fat: 16g
Protein: 6g
Carbohydrates: 31g

Ingredients:

- Beef chuck or rump roast, boneless, weighing 1 pound
- ½ tsp of freshly ground black pepper
- 1 ½ of olive oil
- ½ of a tiny, chopped sweet onion
- 2 tbsp of minced garlic
- 1 tsp of thyme, dried
- 1 cup of water plus 3 teaspoons
- 2 tbsp of cornstarch

Instructions:

- Over medium heat, put a big stockpot.
- Adding pepper to the roast will enhance the flavor.
- In a stockpot, heat the oil and brown the meat on both sides.
- Scoop the meat out onto a platter and put it aside.
- For approximately three minutes, or until softened, sauté the onion and garlic in the stockpot.
- Add the thyme and 1 cup water to the saucepan, along with the meat and any collected juices.
- In order to prevent the liquid from scorching, bring it to a boil and then turn the heat down to low.
- When the meat is quite soft, after approximately 4 ½ hours of simmering, remove the lid.
- Cornstarch and 3 tablespoons of water should be mixed together in a small dish to make a slurry.
- For a thicker sauce, simmer the slurry dissolved in the liquid for 15 minutes, whisking constantly.
- Toss the meat in the gravy and serve.

Beef Stew, Roasted

Preparation Time: 30 Minutes
Servings: 3

Nutritional Analysis:
Total Calories: 249
Total fat: 6g
Protein: 9g
Carbohydrates: 35g

Ingredients:
- ¼ cup of all-purpose flour
- 1 tsp of finely powdered black pepper, plus more for taste
- Shake in some chili pepper
- 1-inch cubes of boneless beef chuck roast, after being shaved of fat
- 2 tbsp of olive oil
- 2 medium-sized sweet onion, diced
- 2 tbsp of minced garlic equaling
- 1 cup of homemade beef stock
- Add 2 tablespoons of water to the 1 cup you have.
- 0.5-inch cubes of one carrot
- The greens from 2 celery stalks, chopped
- 1 tsp of fresh thyme
- 1 tbsp of cornstarch
- 2 tsp of chopped fresh parsley

Instructions:
- Get the oven up to temperature, preferably 350 °F.
- Flour, black pepper, and cayenne pepper should be combined in a big plastic freezer bag and shaken well to combine.
- Put the beef pieces in a plastic bag and toss them around so they're well coated.
- Olive oil should be heated in a big ovenproof saucepan.
- In a skillet over medium heat, brown the beef cubes for approximately 5 minutes.
- Take the steak out of the stew and place it on a serving platter.
- For three minutes, sauté the onion and garlic after adding them to the saucepan.

- Deglaze the pan with the beef stock and scrape the browned pieces off the bottom with a wooden spoon.
- Mix in the carrot, celery, and thyme with the meat drippings on the dish, along with 1 cup of water.
- Put the saucepan into the oven and cover it with a lid or aluminum foil.
- Stirring the stew periodically while baking for approximately an hour should ensure the meat is fork-tender.
- Pull the stew out of the oven.
- To thicken the sauce, combine the cornstarch and 2 tablespoons of water in a small dish and whisk until smooth.
- Add some black pepper to the stew and sprinkle some parsley on top before serving.

Kebabs With Beef and Vegetables

Preparation Time: 30 Minutes
Servings: 1

Nutritional Analysis:
Total Calories: 279
Total fat: 11g
Protein: 15g
Carbohydrates: 40g

Ingredients:

- ½ cup of brown rice
- 2 ½ oz of water
- 4 oz of prime ribeye (choice)
- ¼ tsp of low-calorie Italian dressing
- A single green pepper, seeded and sliced into quarters
- 4 little tomatoes
- ¼ of an onion, diced into 4 wedges

Instructions:

- 2 skewers, either metal or wet wooden ones (for 30 minutes)
- The rice and water should be cooked together in a pot over high heat. Get the water boiling. Once the water has been absorbed and the rice is soft, which should take approximately 30 to 45 minutes, reduce the heat to low, cover, and simmer. To prevent the rice from drying out, add extra liquid if required. Put in a small dish and set aside to keep heated.
- Divide the meat into four servings. Combine the meat and Italian dressing in a small dish and set aside. Coat each slice with the dressing. Marinate for at least twenty minutes in the fridge, rotating once.
- Get a grill going using charcoal, gas, or the broiler, and get the heat up. Lightly spray the grill rack or broiler pan away from the heat source. Cooking rack should be 4–6 inches away from the fire.

Spicy Breasts of Chicken

Preparation Time: 30 Minutes
Servings: 2

Nutritional Analysis:
Total Calories: 250
Total fat: 10g
Protein: 26g
Carbohydrates: 44g

Ingredients:

- 1 cup of yellow onion, minced
- 4 minced garlic cloves
- ½ tsp of canola oil
- Brown rice, prepared to a one-cup serving
- 1-pound of ground chicken breast
- 2 tbsp of fennel seed
- 1 tbsp of cumin seed (or caraway, which has a milder flavor)
- 1 tsp of paprika, ground
- ½ onion, diced
- 1 tsp ground black pepper
- ½ tsp of white pepper
- a pinch of ground cayenne pepper
- ¼ tsp of dried or 1 tsp of fresh chopped rosemary
- 14 tsp of ground nutmeg
- 1 tsp of ground mustard seed
- 1 tsp of celery seed

Instructions:

- Sauté the onion and garlic in the canola oil until the onion is caramelized and the garlic is fragrant. Place in a large bowl and stir in the ground chicken, cooked rice, and the rest of the ingredients. To chill in the fridge for 1 hour.
- Separate the ingredients into 6 equal pieces. Form into a link of sausage. You may also use a piping bag and six sausage shapes to make the mixture. Put on a flat pan or sheet.
- Bake for 5-10 minutes at 350 °F, or until the internal temperature reaches 125 °F. Then finish cooking on the grill. Cook the sausages until they reach an internal

temperature of 165 °F.

- Put two meat cubes, two pieces of pepper, two cherry tomatoes, and two onion wedges on each skewer. To cook the kebabs, put them on the grilling rack or a broiler pan. Cook the kebabs on a grill or under the broiler for 5-10 minutes, rotating occasionally.
- Assign portions of rice to each person's plate. One kebab should be placed on top and the dish should be served right away.

Beef Rollups in Tortillas

Preparation Time: 40 Minutes
Servings: 1

Nutritional Analysis:
Total Calories: 290
Total fat: 15g
Protein: 18g
Carbohydrates: 40g

Ingredients:
- 2-inch flour tortillas (2)
- 2 tsp of cream cheese, whipped
- 5 oz of cooked roast beef
- ¼ cup of chopped onion
- ¼ of a red, yellow, or green sweet bell pepper, sliced into strips
- 8 cubed cucumbers

Instructions:
- Coat tortillas with cream cheese.
- Wrap each tortilla with a half of the roast beef, half of the red onion, half of the pepper strips, half of the cucumber, and half of the lettuce.
- Constrain your muscles and kink them up like a jelly roll.
- Each tortilla may be cut into quarters or served as is. Romaine lettuce leaves

Chapter 6: Fish and Seafood Recipes

Calamari with Herbs and Lemon, Grilled

Preparation Time: 20 Minutes
Servings: 2

Nutritional Analysis:
Total Calories: 244
Total fat: 15g
Protein: 16g
Carbohydrates: 40g

Ingredients:

- 2 tsp of olive oil
- 2 tsp of lemon juice, freshly squeezed
- 1 tbsp of fresh parsley, minced
- 1 tbsp of finely chopped fresh oregano
- 2 tbsp of minced garlic
- Sprinkle on some finely powdered black pepper
- A half pound of squid, after cleaning
- Slices of lemon for garnish

Instructions:

- Mix the lemon juice, olive oil, parsley, oregano, garlic, salt, and pepper in a large bowl.
- Drop the calamari rings into the basin and toss to coat.
- Put a lid on the bowl and marinate the calamari in the fridge for an hour.
- Get the grill nice and toasty.
- The calamari should be grilled for approximately 3 minutes, flipping once, until it is firm and opaque.
- Serve with lemon wedges

Tuna with Pesto and Herbs

Preparation Time: 20 Minutes
Servings: 1

Nutritional Analysis:
Total Calories: 219
Total fat: 10g
Protein: 16g
Carbohydrates: 36g

Ingredients:
- 4 yellowfin tuna fillets (about 3 ounces each)
- 1 tsp of olive oil
- Cracked black pepper, just ground
- 1/3 tsp herb pesto
- 1 lemon, sliced into 8 thin slices

Instructions:
- Prepare a medium-high flame in the grill.
- Sprinkle some pepper on each fish fillet and drizzle it with olive oil.
- The fish should take 4 minutes to cook on the grill.
- Turn the fish over and top each piece with the herb pesto and lemon wedges.
- Grill for 5 to 6 minutes longer or until the tuna is cooked too medium-well. Serve immediately

Fish with Cilantro and Lime

Preparation Time: 30 Minutes
Servings: 3

Nutritional Analysis:
Total Calories: 219
Total fat: 10g
Protein: 16g
Carbohydrates: 47g

Ingredients:
- 14 cup of mayonnaise
- 1 lime's juice
- 1 lime's worth of zest
- ½ cup of fresh, chopped cilantro
- 3 pounds of flounder cut into 4 fillets
- Cracked black pepper, just ground

Instructions:
- Turn the oven temperature up to 400 °F.
- Blend mayonnaise, lime juice, lime zest, and cilantro in a little bowl.
- Arrange four squares of foil, each measuring approximately 8 inches by 8 inches, on a tidy table.
- Each square should have a fillet of flounder placed in the middle.
- Use the mayonnaise mixture to coat the fillets evenly.
- Pepper the flounder before cooking.
- Create a sealed pouch by folding the edges of the foil over the fish, then placing the
- Packs in foil on a baking pan.
- Fish needs around 5 minutes in the oven.
- To serve, unfold the packages.

Sole Fillets

Preparation Time: 35 Minutes
Servings: 1

Nutritional Analysis:
Total Calories: 288
Total fat: 10g
Protein: 5g
Carbohydrates: 40g

Ingredients:
- ¼ cup of all-purpose flour
- A pinch of freshly ground black pepper
- 12 oz of sole fillets, peeled and boned
- 2 tbsp of olive oil
- 1 scallion, chopped green and white
- Slices of lemon for garnish

Instructions:
- Flour and black pepper should be combined in a big plastic freezer bag and shaken until well mixed.
- Fish fillets may be coated with flour by being added and then shaken in the jar.
- Warm the olive oil in a large pan set over medium heat.
- Fry the sole fillets for approximately 5 minutes, flipping once, or until golden and cooked through, after the oil is heated.
- The fish should be drained on paper towels after being taken out of the oil.
- Sprinkle with sliced scallions and fresh squeezed lemon juice before serving.

Fish and Chips

Preparation Time: 20 Minutes
Servings: 3

Nutritional Analysis:
Total Calories: 219
Total fat: 17g
Protein: 16g
Carbohydrates: 30g

Ingredients:

- 2 cups of eggplant, sliced into ½ -inch cubes after being peeled
- Margarine, to coat the baking dish with
- 1 ½ tsp of olive oil
- ½ of a tiny, chopped sweet onion
- 1 tsp of chopped garlic
- 1 sliced celery stalk
- ½ red bell pepper, cooked and diced
- 3 tsp of freshly squeezed lemon juice
- 1/10 of chili pepper sauce
- ¼ of creole seasoning mix
- ½ cup of uncooked white rice
- 1 large egg
- 4 oz of shrimp, cooked

Instructions:

- Get the oven up to temperature, preferably 350 °F.
- The ingredients should be boiled in a small pot of water over medium heat.
- Cooking time of 5 minutes is sufficient for eggplant. Empty the contents of the dish and put aside.
- Prepare a 9-by-13-inch baking dish for later use by greasing it with butter.
- Olive oil should be heated in a big pan over moderate heat.
- Prepare the onion, garlic, celery, and bell pepper by sautéing them for 4 minutes.
- The meat is quite soft.
- Sauté the veggies, then add them to the eggplant along with the hot lemon juice.

- Rice, a fried egg, Creole spice, and sauce. pounds of king crab
- Blend the ingredients together by mixing.
- Combine the seafood by folding it in.
- Distribute the casserole filling among casserole dishes and smooth the top with a spoon.
- Put the casserole into the oven, and bake for 25 to 30 minutes, or until it is hot throughout and the
- The rice is soft and delicious.
- Serve hot.

Salmon with a Sugary Glaze

Preparation Time: 30 Minutes
Servings: 4

Nutritional Analysis:
Total Calories: 229
Total fat: 10g
Protein: 7g
Carbohydrates: 30g

Ingredients:

- 2 tbsp of honey
- ¼ of a lemon grated
- ½ tsp of freshly ground black pepper
- For four people, prepare four salmon fillets (each weighing three ounces).
- 1 ½ of olive oil
- ½ scallion, chopped (both the white and green sections)

Instructions:

- Mix the honey, lemon juice, and pepper in a small bowl.
- Dry the salmon with paper towels after washing it.
- Spread the honey-based mixture evenly over the fillets.
- Olive oil should be heated in a big pan over moderate heat.
- After adding the salmon fillets, simmer them for approximately 10 minutes, flipping once, or until they are browned and just cooked through.
- Add sliced scallion as a garnish before serving.

Chapter 7: Vegetable Mains Recipes

Salad of Couscous and Vegetables Dressed with a Spicy Citrus Dressing.

Preparation Time: 25 Minutes
Servings: 1

Nutritional Analysis:
Total Calories: 258
Total fat: 6g
Protein: 9g
Carbohydrates: 30g

Ingredients:

- ¼ mug of olive oil
- 3 tsp of freshly squeezed grapefruit juice
- 1 lime's juice
- 1 lime's worth of zest
- 1 tbsp of fresh parsley, minced
- Shake in some chili pepper
- Cracked black pepper, just ground
- 3 cups of cooled, cooked couscous
- ½ of a red bell pepper, diced
- 1 scallion, including white and green sections, chopped
- 1 apple, cored and cut
- Olive oil, grapefruit juice, lime juice, and salt should be mixed together in a small basin.
- Cayenne pepper, parsley, and lime zest.
- Add black pepper as a seasoning.

Instructions:

- Combine the couscous, red pepper, scallion, and parsley in a large bowl and refrigerate for at least an hour before serving.
- Apple.
- The couscous mixture is complete after the dressing has been added and tossed to blend.
- Put in the fridge and let it chill for at least an hour.

Confetti Salad with Farfalle

Preparation Time: 15 Minutes
Servings: 2

Nutritional Analysis:
Total Calories: 255
Total fat: 16g
Protein: 14g
Carbohydrates: 32g

Ingredients:
- 2 cups of cooked farfalle
- ¼ cup red bell pepper, cooked and coarsely chopped
- ¼ cup coarsely sliced cucumber
- ¼ cup grated carrot
- 2 tbsp chopped yellow bell pepper
- Green half of a scallion, coarsely chopped
- ½ cup of mayonnaise
- 1 tbsp of lemon juice, squeezed
- 1 tsp of finely chopped fresh parsley

Instructions:
- Half a teaspoon of white sugar
- Cracked black pepper, just ground
- Add the spaghetti, red pepper, cucumber, and carrot to a large bowl and toss to combine.
- Scallion with yellow pepper.
- Mix the mayonnaise, lemon juice, parsley, and sugar.
- After the spaghetti and vegetables have been combined, add the dressing and mix well.
- Put some pepper on it.
- Put in the fridge and let it chill for at least an hour.

Tabbouleh

Preparation Time: 10 Minutes
Servings: 2

Nutritional Analysis:
Total Calories: 219
Total fat: 10g
Protein: 16g
Carbohydrates: 30g

Ingredients:
- Approximately 4 cups of white rice, cooked
- 1/2 of a red pepper, cooked and diced
- 1/2 a yellow pepper, cooked and sliced
- 2 cups of zucchini, diced finely, cooked until soft

Instructions:
- One cup of boiling, peeled, and diced eggplant
- 1/4 cup of fresh parsley, chopped
- 1/4 cup of fresh cilantro, chopped
- 2-tablespoons of olive oil
- One lemon's juice

Lemon gratings one

Preparation Time: 25 Minutes
Servings: 1

Nutritional Analysis:
Total Calories: 219
Total fat: 6g
Protein: 12g
Carbohydrates: 35g

Ingredients:

- Cracked black pepper, just ground

Instructions:

- Mix the rice, red bell pepper, yellow bell pepper, zucchini, eggplant, parsley, cilantro, olive oil, lemon juice, and lemon zest in a large bowl.
- Put some pepper on it.
- It's best to refrigerate the salad for at least an hour before serving.

Eggplant and Tofu Stir-Fry

Preparation Time: 20 Minutes
Servings: 2

Nutritional Analysis:
Total Calories: 219
Total fat: 11g
Protein: 8g
Carbohydrates: 35g

Ingredients:

- 1 tbsp of granulated sugar
- 1 tbsp of whole wheat flour
- 1 tsp of fresh ginger, grated
- 1 tsp of chopped garlic
- 1 tsp of jalapeno pepper, minced
- 1 lime's juice
- Water
- 2 tsp of olive oil, to be shared
- Cubed extra-firm tofu (about 5 ounces) measuring 1/2 inch on a side
- 2 cups of cubed eggplant
- 2 scallion, sliced green and white sections
- 3 tbsp of chopped cilantro

Instructions:

- Mix sugar, flour, ginger, garlic, jalapeno, and Reserve after combining lime juice and enough water to produce a sauce measuring 2/3 cup.
- One tablespoon of the oil should be heated in a large pan over medium heat.
- Make sure the tofu is crispy and golden by sautéing it for at least 6 minutes.
- Take out the tofu and put it on a platter.
- For approximately 10 minutes, or until the eggplant cubes are cooked through and gently browned, add the remaining 1 tablespoon oil and sauté them.
- Scallions and tofu should be added to the pan and stirred together.
- Add the sauce, bring to a boil, and cook, stirring often, for 2 minutes, or until the sauce has thickened.
- Before serving, sprinkle on the cilantro.

Recipe for Broccoli and Meatball Mie Goreng

Preparation Time: 20 Minutes
Servings: 3

Nutritional Analysis:
Total Calories: 219
Total fat: 13g
Protein: 7g
Carbohydrates: 38g

Ingredients:

- ½ pound of ramen noodles
- 14 cups of granulated dark brown sugar
- 2 tbsp of minced garlic
- 1 tsp of fresh ginger, grated
- 1 tsp of low-sodium soy sauce
- ½ tsp of sambal Olenek
- Tofu, extremely firm, 4 ounces, cubed, 1/2-inch
- 1 tbsp cornstarch
- 2 tsp of olive oil, to be shared
- 2 cups of broccoli stems removed and florets chopped off
- The green and white sections of 2 scallions, cut very thinly on the diagonal
- Wedge of lime for presentation

Instructions:

- Noodles should be prepared according package directions, drained, and left aside.
- Put the brown sugar, garlic, ginger, soy sauce, and sambal Olenek into a bowl and mix well.
- After 30 minutes, transfer the tofu to a paper towel to drain.
- Combine the cornstarch and tofu in a plastic bag, then shake to get rid of any excess.
- Warm 1 tablespoon of the olive oil in a large pan over medium heat.
- To get the tofu brown and crispy, add it to the pan and cook it for approximately 10 minutes.
- Toss the tofu on a platter using a slotted spoon.
- Put the remaining tablespoon of oil into the pan.
- Broccoli just needs four minutes in the pan to get soft.
- Put the sauce and the tofu in a pan and heat it for 2 minutes, or until the tofu is heated through.
- This sauce is becoming thicker.
- Add scallions and lime wedges before serving.

Salsa de Lime and Cucumber with Grilled Shrimp

Preparation Time: 25 Minutes
Servings: 3

Nutritional Analysis:
Total Calories: 229
Total fat: 14g
Protein: 16g
Carbohydrates: 30g

Ingredients:

- 2 tbsp of olive oil
- 16-20 big shrimp, about 6 ounces total, peeled and deveined with the tails on
- 1 tsp of chopped garlic
- ½ cup of finely diced English cucumber
- 2 cups of diced mango
- 1 lime's worth of zest
- 1 lime's juice
- Cracked black pepper, just ground
- Wedge of lime for presentation
- Put four wooden skewers in water for 30 minutes.

Instructions:

- Turn the grill heat up to medium-high.
- Combine the shrimp, garlic, and olive oil in a large bowl and toss to combine.
- You should use roughly four shrimp per skewer.
- Combine the diced cucumber, diced mango, lime zest, lime juice, and a pinch of pepper in a small bowl and toss to combine. Don't bother with right now.
- The shrimp are done when they are opaque all the way through and have been grilled for approximately 10 minutes with one rotation.
- Pepper the shrimp very lightly.
- Plating suggestion: shrimp on cucumber salsa, with lime wedges on the side.

Linguine with Shrimp Scampi

Preparation Time: 25 Minutes
Servings: 2

Nutritional Analysis:
Total Calories: 219
Total fat: 10g
Protein: 16g
Carbohydrates: 33g

Ingredients:

- 4 oz uncooked linguine
- 1 tsp of olive oil
- 2 tbsp of minced garlic
- 4 ounces of shrimp, cleaned, deveined, and cut
- ½ cup of white wine, dry
- 1 lemon's juice
- 1 tbsp of fresh basil, chopped
- ½ cup of thick cream

Instructions:

- Cracked black pepper, just ground
- Pasta should be prepared per package directions, then drained and left aside.
- Olive oil should be heated in a big pan over moderate heat.
- For approximately 6 minutes, or until the shrimp is pink, sauté the garlic and shrimp in the olive oil.
- Just-cooked and opaqueness.
- After 5 minutes, stir in the wine, lemon juice, and basil and continue cooking.
- After 2 minutes of simmering, add the cream and stir to combine.
- Drop the linguine into the pan and stir to coat.
- The spaghetti should be served in four servings.

Lime Salsa with Crab Cakes

Preparation Time: 25 Minutes
Servings: 3

Nutritional Analysis:
Total Calories: 249
Total fat: 10g
Protein: 6g
Carbohydrates: 35g

Ingredients:

- ½ English cucumber, diced
- 1 lime, diced
- ½ cup red bell pepper, cooked and diced
- 1 tsp of chopped fresh cilantro
- Cracked black pepper, just ground
- 8 oz of queen crab flesh
- 14 cups of dry bread crumbs
- 1 little egg
- Pepper, red, quarter cup, cooked and diced
- In a food processor, mince 1 scallion (both the green and white portions).
- 1 tbsp of fresh parsley, minced
- Squirt some chili sauce on it
- For the pan, olive oil spray

Instructions:

- Combine the cucumber, lime juice, red pepper, and cilantro in a small bowl and toss to combine.
- Pepper it and put it away for later use.
- Crab, bread crumbs, egg, red pepper, scallion, parsley, and spicy sauce are mixed together until a ball form in a medium basin. If extra bread crumbs are needed, add them.
- Make 4 patties out of the crab mixture and set them out to enjoy.
- You may firm up the crab cakes by putting them in the fridge for an hour.
- Put a big skillet on the stove over medium heat and coat it liberally with olive oil spray.
- If you're cooking the crab cakes all at once, they'll take too long to brown on both sides.
- Toss some salsa with the crab cakes and serve.

Vegetables in Cucumber Wraps

Preparation Time: 20 Minutes

Servings: 3

Nutritional Analysis:

Total Calories: 22

Total fat: 10g

Protein: 9g

Carbohydrates: 25g

Ingredients:

- 2 cups of finely shredded red cabbage
- ½ cup of grated carrot
- ¼ red bell pepper, cut into julienne strips
- 14 cups of finely chopped cilantro
- 1 ½ tsp of olive oil
- ¼ tsp of ground cumin
- A pinch of freshly ground black pepper

Instructions:

- Using a vegetable peeler, cut one English cucumber into eight paper-thin ribbons.
- Combine the cabbage, carrot, red pepper, scallion, cilantro, olive oil, cumin, and black pepper in a medium bowl and toss to combine.
- Put a little amount of the veggie filling towards one end of each cucumber strip and split it evenly.
- Secure the stuffed cucumber rolls with a wooden pick by rolling them up.
- It should be done again with each individual cucumber strip.

Vegetable Curry with a Thai Twist

Preparation Time: 15 Minutes
Servings: 2

Nutritional Analysis:
Total Calories: 219
Total fat: 13g
Protein: 8g
Carbohydrates: 41g

Ingredients:

- 2 tsp of olive oil
- ½ of sweet onion, chopped
- 2 tbsp of minced garlic
- 2 tsp of grated fresh ginger
- ½ cup of chopped, peeled eggplant
- 1 peeled and sliced carrot
- 1 chopped red bell pepper
- 2 tbsp of spicy curry
- 1 tsp of cumin seed powder
- ½ tsp of ground coriander
- Shake in some chili pepper
- 2 cups of fresh, home-made vegetable stock
- 1 tbsp cornstarch

Instructions:

- Water equivalent to a quarter cup
- Oil should be heated in a large stockpot over medium heat.
- Onion, garlic, and ginger need 3 minutes in a hot pan to soften.
- For another 6 minutes of sautéing, frequently mix in the eggplant, carrots, and red pepper.
- Mix in the vegetable stock, curry powder, cumin, coriander, cayenne pepper, and salt.
- Get the curry boiling, then turn the heat down low.
- For tender veggies, simmer the curry for at least 30 minutes.
- Combining the cornstarch and water in a little bowl.
- Simmer the curry for approximately 5 minutes after stirring in the cornstarch mixture.

Cooked Rice with Vegetables

Preparation Time: 25 Minutes
Servings: 3

Nutritional Analysis:
Total Calories: 29
Total fat: 6g
Protein: 9g
Carbohydrates: 25g

Ingredients:
- 2 medium-sized sweet onion, diced
- 1 tbsp of freshly grated ginger
- 2 tbsp of minced garlic
- 1 cup of carrots, cut
- ½ cup of eggplant, chopped
- ½ cup of peas
- 2 cups of green beans, sliced into 1-inch pieces
- 2 tsp of finely chopped fresh coriander
- 3 cups of finished rice

Instructions:
- Warm the olive oil in a large pan set over medium heat.
- To soften the onion, ginger, and garlic, sauté them for approximately 3 minutes.
- Then, after another 3 minutes of sautéing, mix in the carrot, eggplant, peas, and green beans.
- Mix the rice and cilantro together.
- For approximately 10 minutes, or until the rice is warm, sauté it while stirring regularly.
- Dish up right away.

Chapter 8: Snacks and Appetizers Recipes

Rice That Has Been Fried

Preparation Time: 30 Minutes
Servings: 4

Nutritional Analysis:
Total Calories: 259
Total fat: 10g
Protein: 16g
Carbohydrates: 50g

Ingredients:

- 2 cups of brown rice
- 3 tbsp of peanut oil
- 4 green onions, including the greens, cut
- 2 carrots, cut very small
- ½ cup of green bell peppers, cut coarsely
- 2 to 3 cups of frozen peas
- 1 egg
- 2 tsp of reduced-sodium soy sauce
- 1 tbsp of Sesame Oil

Instructions:

- Incorporating a Parsley Sprig
- Peanut oil should be heated over medium heat in a big, heavy pan or wok. Sauté the cooked rice until it just begins to turn golden. Toss in some peas, carrots, green pepper, and onions. Cook in a wok for approximately 5 minutes, or until the veggies are crisp-tender.
- Push the rice and veggies to the edges of the pan to create a hollow in the middle. Scramble the egg as it cooks after being broken into the hollow. Mix the egg scramble into the rice. Blend soy sauce, sesame oil, and chopped parsley and sprinkle over top. Dish up right away.

Hot Grain Cereal

Preparation Time: 20 Minutes
Servings: 2

Nutritional Analysis:
Total Calories: 209
Total fat: 13g
Protein: 11g
Carbohydrates: 40g

Ingredients:
- ½ cup of uncooked pearl barley and red wheat berries
- ½ cup of brown rice in its uncooked form
- ¼ cup of steel-cut oats, raw
- 3 tbsp quinoa, uncooked
- 2 tbsp of flaxseed oil

Instructions:
- Approximately one and a half quarts of water
- Mix the barley, wheat berries, rice, oats, quinoa, flaxseed in a large pot. Combine all ingredients in a pot and bring to a boil over medium heat, then whisk in water. For 45 minutes, with occasional tossing, keep the heat on low and simmer the mixture.

Dip with Roasted Onion and Garlic

Preparation Time: 20 Minutes
Servings: 2

Nutritional Analysis:
Total Calories: 200
Total fat: 8g
Protein: 6g
Carbohydrates: 20g

Ingredients:

- 8 thin slices from 1 big sweet onion, after peeling
- 8 cloves of garlic
- 2 tsp of olive oil
- ½ cup of light sour cream,
- ½ tsp of dried ginger
- 1 tsp of fresh parsley, minced
- 1 tsp of fresh thyme
- Cracked black pepper, just ground

Instructions:

- Bring the oven up to 425 °F.
- Combine the olive oil and the onion and garlic in a small bowl.
- Toss the sliced onion and garlic cloves onto a sheet of aluminum foil loosely wrapped veggies
- Bake the foil packet in the oven by placing it on a small baking sheet.
- Cook the veggies in the oven for 50 minutes to 1 hour, or until they have a strong aroma and gleaming with gold.
- Take the package out of the oven and let it cool for fifteen minutes.
- Combine the sour cream, lemon juice, parsley, and garlic in a medium bowl and mix well.
- The combination of thyme and black pepper.
- Carefully remove the veggies from the foil and set them down on a chopping board.
- Add the chopped veggies to the sour cream. Blend to combine.
- It's best to cover the dip and chill it for at least an hour in the fridge before serving.

"Baba Ghanoush"

Preparation Time: 10 Minutes
Servings: 2

Nutritional Analysis:
Total Calories: 200
Total fat: 11g
Protein: 10g
Carbohydrates: 12g

Ingredients:
- 1 medium eggplant, sliced in half lengthwise, with the halves scored in a crosshatch pattern
- 1 tbsp of olive oil, with more for brushing
- 1 large sweet onion, diced and peeled
- 2 cloves of garlic, cut in half
- 1 tsp of cumin seed powder
- 1 tsp of ground coriander
- 1 tbsp of lemon juice
- Cracked black pepper, just ground

Instructions:
- Turn the oven temperature up to 400 °F.
- Spread parchment paper out on two baking sheets.
- Coat the cut sides of the eggplant halves with olive oil and spread them out on a baking sheet.
- Onion, garlic, 1 tbsp olive oil, cumin, and coriander should be combined in a separate small bowl.
- On the second baking sheet, distribute the seasoned onions.
- Roast the onions for 20 minutes and the eggplant for 30, or until softened and browned.
- Take them out of the oven and use a spoon to scoop the eggplant meat onto a basin.
- On a chopping board, roughly chop the onions and garlic, then add them.
- It's the eggplant, of course.
- Pepper and lemon juice and stir.
- Hot or cold, serve it whichever you want.

Herb-and-Cheese Spread

Preparation Time: 15 Minutes
Servings: 2

Nutritional Analysis:
Total Calories: 219
Total fat: 10g
Protein: 16g
Carbohydrates: 30g

Ingredients:

- 1 cup worth of cream cheese
- ½ cup of rice milk, unsweetened
- ½ green scallion, coarsely chopped
- 1 tbsp of fresh parsley, minced
- 1 tbsp of fresh basil, chopped;
- 1 tbsp of Lemon Juice, Squeezed
- 1 tsp of chopped garlic

Instructions:

- 50 milligrams of fresh thyme, chopped
- A pinch of freshly ground black pepper
- Combine the cream cheese, milk, scallion, parsley, basil, lemon juice, garlic, thyme, and pepper in a medium bowl.
- Keep the dip in the fridge for up to a week in an airtight container.

Fried Kale Chips with a Kick

Preparation Time: 20 Minutes
Servings: 2

Nutritional Analysis:
Total Calories: 219
Total fat: 10g
Protein: 6g
Carbohydrates: 35g

Ingredients:
- 2 cups of kale
- 2 tsp of olive oil
- A pinch of chili powder
- Shake in some chili pepper

Instructions:
- Turn the oven temperature up to 300 °F.
- Prepare two baking sheets in advance by lining them with parchment paper.
- Pull the kale leaves away from the stems and shred them into pieces about 2 inches in size.
- Kale should be washed and patted dry.
- Toss the greens with some olive oil in a big bowl.
- Massage the oil into the kale with your hands, being sure to cover each leaf.
- Add the spices (chili powder and cayenne pepper) and toss the kale to evenly distribute them.
- The seasoned kale should be spread out in a single layer on each baking sheet. Don't bunch the leaves together.
- In a preheated oven at 400 degrees, bake the kale until it is dry and crisp, about 20 to 25 minutes.
- After 5 minutes, take the trays out of the oven and let the chips cool there.
- Dish up right away.

Tortilla Chips with Cinnamon

Preparation Time: 25 Minutes
Servings: 2

Nutritional Analysis:
Total Calories: 270
Total fat: 9g
Protein: 12g
Carbohydrates: 25g

Ingredients:

- 2 tbsp granulated sugar
- ½ tsp of cinnamon powder
- A pinch of crush nutmeg
- 3 to 6 inches of tortillas flour

Instructions:

- To spray the tortillas with cooking spray before baking
- Get the oven up to temperature, preferably 350 °F.
- Put parchment paper on a baking pan.
- Combine the sugar, cinnamon, and nutmeg in a small bowl and mix well.
- Spread the tortillas out on a dry surface and coat both sides with cooking spray.
- Cover both sides of each tortilla with the cinnamon sugar.
- Spread the tortillas out on a baking pan after cutting each one into 16 wedges.
- Crisp up the tortilla wedges in the oven, flipping once, for approximately 10 minutes.
- After cooling, chips may be kept for a week in an airtight container at room temperature.

Gourmet Kettle Corn with a Sweet and Spicy Coating

Preparation Time: 35 Minutes
Servings: 2

Nutritional Analysis:
Total Calories: 219
Total fat: 5g
Protein: 16g
Carbohydrates: 30g

Ingredients:
- 3 Tbsp of olive oil
- 1 cup of popcorn kernels
- 2 cups of dark sugar

Instructions:
- Shake in some chili pepper
- Put a few popcorn kernels and the olive oil in a big, covered saucepan and cook it over medium heat.
- To get the popcorn popping, give the saucepan a little shake. Put the remaining kernels and sugar in the saucepan.
- Put the cover on the saucepan and shake it vigorously until all the kernels have popped.
- Take the popcorn out of the saucepan and into a big bowl, then turn off the heat.
- Stir in the cayenne pepper and serve over popcorn.

Ice Pops with Blueberries and Cream

Preparation Time: 30 Minutes
Servings: 2

Nutritional Analysis:
Total Calories: 219
Total fat: 10g
Protein: 9g
Carbohydrates: 30g

Ingredients:

- 3 cups of fresh blueberries
- 1 tsp of freshly squeezed lemon juice
- ¼ cup rice milk, unsweetened
- ¼ cup reduced-fat sour cream
- ¼ cup of white sugar
- ½ tsp of natural vanilla essence
- ¼ tsp of cinnamon powder

Instructions:

- In a blender or food processor, combine the blueberries, sugar, sour cream, vanilla, and rice milk.
- Put the cinnamon and combine it until it's a smooth paste.
- Scoop the mixture into ice pop molds and freeze for at least three hours, preferably overnight.

Candy Ginger with Frozen Milk

Preparation Time: 20 Minutes
Servings: 1

Nutritional Analysis:
Total Calories: 200
Total fat: 13g
Protein: 9g
Carbohydrates: 10g

Ingredients:

- 4 glasses of rice milk flavored with vanilla
- ½ cup of white sugar, granulated
- 1 piece of fresh ginger (about 4 inches long) with its peelings, thinly sliced
- ¼ of ground nutmeg
- ¼ cup of candied ginger, chopped

Instructions:

- Milk, sugar, and fresh ginger should be combined in a large pot and warmed-over medium heat, stirring often.
- Stirring periodically, bring the milk mixture to nearly a boil over the course of 5 minutes.
- Reduce to a gentle simmer and let cook for 15 minutes.
- Turn off the heat and stir in the ground nutmeg to the milk. Allow the ingredients to rest together for an hour to allow the flavors to combine.
- After combining the milk and ginger, strain it through a fine sieve into a medium basin to remove the ginger.
- You may now add the candied ginger and chill the mixture in the fridge.
- Follow the directions provided by your ice cream maker to freeze the ginger ice.
- The completed dessert may be kept frozen for up to three months if stored in an airtight container.

Delicious Meringue Cookies

Preparation Time: 25 Minutes
Servings: 1

Nutritional Analysis:
Total Calories: 279
Total fat: 16g
Protein: 6g
Carbohydrates: 21g

Ingredients:

- 4 egg whites at room temperature
- 1 cup of granulated sugar
- 1 tsp of vanilla extract
- 1 tsp of almond essence

Instructions:

- Turn the oven temperature up to 300 °F.
- Set aside 2 baking sheets that have been lined with parchment paper.
- Egg whites should be beaten until firm peaks form in a large stainless-steel basin.
- To make a thick and glossy meringue, add the granulated sugar a tablespoon at a time, beating thoroughly after each addition.
- Vanilla and almond extracts should be beaten in at this point.
- Scoop tablespoonfuls of the meringue batter and put them onto the prepared baking pans, leaving a little of room between each cookie.
- If you want your cookies crunchy, bake them for another 5-10 minutes.
- Take the cookies out of the oven and let them cool on wire racks.
- The cookies may be kept for a week at room temperature if stored in an airtight container.

Antojitos

Preparation Time: 10 Minutes
Servings: 1

Nutritional Analysis:
Total Calories: 219
Total fat: 10g
Protein: 10g
Carbohydrates: 30g

Ingredients:

- 6 oz plain cream cheese, softened at room temperature
- ½ of a jalapeno pepper, cut finely
- ½ of a sliced scallion (greens alone)
- ¼ cup of red bell pepper, diced
- ½ tsp of ground cumin
- ½ tsp of dried coriander seed
- ½ tsp of chili powder
- 3 corn tortillas, 8 inches in diameter

Instructions:

- Cream cheese, jalapeno pepper, scallion, red bell pepper, cumin, coriander, and chili powder should be combined in a medium bowl.
- Spread the cream cheese mixture thinly over three tortillas, reserving a quarter-inch of tortilla around the edges for rolling, and divide the mixture equally.
- In order to store the tortillas, roll them up like jelly rolls and then wrap them individually in plastic.
- The rolls need to chill in the fridge for at least an hour to solidify.
- Roll up a tortilla, slice it into 1-inch pieces, and serve.

Sauce Made from Roasted Red Peppers and Basil Served Over Linguine

Preparation Time: 30 Minutes
Servings: 1

Nutritional Analysis:
Total Calories: 222
Total fat: 13g
Protein: 9g
Carbohydrates: 33g

Ingredients:

- 8 oz of linguine, raw
- 1 tsp of olive oil
- 2 medium-sized sweet onion, diced
- 2 tbsp of minced garlic
- 1 cup of roasted red bell peppers, diced
- ¼ tsp of balsamic vinegar

Instructions:

- Garnish with the basil and serve.
- Tease out some crushed red pepper
- Cracked black pepper, just ground
- Grated low-fat Parmesan cheese, about 4 teaspoons.
- Pasta should be prepared according package directions.
- In the time it takes the pasta to cook, heat the olive oil in a large pan over medium heat.
- To soften the onions and garlic, sauté them for approximately 3 minutes.
- For approximately 5 minutes, or until the red pepper, vinegar, basil, and red pepper flakes are hot, mix everything together in a pan.
- Pepper the spaghetti before tossing it with the sauce.
- Use grated Parmesan as a finishing touch.

Recipe for Baked Macaroni and Cheese

Preparation Time: 35 Minutes
Servings: 3

Nutritional Analysis:
Total Calories: 249
Total fat: 10g
Protein: 16g
Carbohydrates: 45g

Ingredients:

- Margarine, to coat the baking dish with
- 1 tsp of olive oil
- 2 medium-sized sweet onion, diced
- 1 tsp of chopped garlic
- 1/3 mug soy milk
- 1 cup worth of cream cheese
- ½ tsp of ground mustard
- ½ tsp of freshly ground black pepper

Instructions:

- Shake in some chili pepper
- Macaroni, enough for 3 cups once cooked.
- Prepare a 9x9-inch baking dish by greasing it with butter and setting it aside.
- Olive oil should be heated over moderate heat in a medium saucepan.
- To soften the onion and garlic, sauté them for approximately 3 minutes.
- Add the milk, cheese, mustard, black pepper, and cayenne pepper and stir until the cheese is melted and the mixture is smooth.
- There are no rough spots in this combination.
- Mix in the macaroni that has already been cooked.
- The dish should be filled with the ingredients and baked immediately after.
- If you like bouncy macaroni, bake it for around 15 minutes.

Fried Egg and Grilled Kale Sandwich

Preparation Time: 40 Minutes
Servings: 1

Nutritional Analysis:
Total Calories: 289
Total fat: 10g
Protein: 16g
Carbohydrates: 41g

Ingredients:

- 2 large kale leaves
- Tease out some crushed red pepper
- 4 tsp of unsalted butter, divided
- 2 pieces of white bread
- 2 tbsp of cream cheese
- 2tiny eggs
- Cracked black pepper, just ground

Instructions:

- Get the oven up to temperature, preferably 350 °F.
- Rub the olive oil into the kale leaves until they are well saturated.
- The kale leaves would benefit from a little dusting of red pepper flakes.
- To make the leaves crispy, put them in a pie pan and bake at 400 °F for approximately 10 minutes.
- The greens should be taken out of the oven and placed aside.
- Coat each piece of bread with butter (one teaspoon's worth) on both sides.
- Toasted bread is best, so heat a large pan over medium heat and toast the bread on both sides for
- Or until it reaches a golden-brown color, which should take around 3 minutes.
- Take the bread out of the pan and put a spoonful of cream cheese on each piece.
- To cook the eggs, melt the remaining 2 tablespoons of butter in the pan.
- Warm and toasty for around four minutes with the sun shining on top.
- Top each piece of bread with some cream cheese, then a fried egg, and some crispy kale.
- Add pepper before serving.

Pizzeria's Famous Grilled Chicken Pita Pizza

Preparation Time: 20 Minutes
Servings: 3

Nutritional Analysis:
Total Calories: 239
Total fat: 5g
Protein: 16g
Carbohydrates: 40g

Ingredients:
- A 6-1/2-inch pita and another pita of the same size
- 3 tsp of reduced-sodium barbecue sauce
- ¼ of a purple onion
- 2 tbsp of crumbled feta
- 4 oz of pre-cooked chicken
- 1/8 tsp of garlic powder

Instructions:
- Set oven temperature to 350 °F.
- Two pita breads should be placed on a baking pan that has been sprayed with nonstick cooking spray.
- Each pita should have around 1 1/2 tablespoons of barbecue sauce spread on it.
- Sprinkle some chopped onion on top of a pita bread.
- Chicken pitas may be made using chicken cut into cubes.
- Pitas should have feta cheese and garlic powder sprinkled on top.
- Put in the oven and set the timer for 11-13 minutes.

The Brewery's Burger

Preparation Time: 25 Minutes
Servings: 1

Nutritional Analysis:
Total Calories: 267
Total fat: 15g
Protein: 10g
Carbohydrates: 20g

Ingredients:

- 1 ½ tbsp of rice milk
- 5 salt-free soda crackers
- 1 large egg
- 1 tsp of seasoning mix of herbs, no salt added
- An ounce of 85% lean ground beef

Instructions:

- You may make a tasty milkshake by mixing some crushed soda crackers with milk. Hold off on snacking until crackers have softened.
- Whip an egg and add it to the cracker crumbs. Combine the herb mixture with the crackers and stir well. When using ground beef, add it and combine well.
- Form the meat mixture into 4 identical patties.
- Cook over a medium flame until an instant-read thermometer registers 160 degrees Fahrenheit.
- Eat as is, on a bun, or top with your favorite condiments and side dishes.

Nachos With Crunchy Chicken

Preparation Time: 40 Minutes
Servings: 2

Nutritional Analysis:
Total Calories: 225
Total fat: 14g
Protein: 9g
Carbohydrates: 23g

Ingredients:

- 1 stalk of celery
- 1 carrot, around medium size
- 1/2 pound of red pepper
- 14 cups of reduced-fat mayonnaise
- A spice mix with onion powder, half a teaspoon
- 2 pieces of lavash made from whole wheat
- 8 ounces of canned chicken with less sodium

Instructions:

- Cut the celery, carrot, and bell pepper into small cubes.
- In a small dish, mix together the onion powder and mayonnaise.
- Spread the mixture on each lavash flatbread using 2 teaspoons.
- Dice the veggies and mix them together in a separate dish.
- On one side of each flatbread, spread 4 ounces of chicken and half of the veggies.
- Make a roll out of the flatbread and slice it in half on the diagonal. Use a toothpick to hold each piece together.
- Cut each tortilla roll in half lengthwise and use a toothpick to secure the halves together.

Quesadillas with Camarones

Preparation Time: 25 Minutes
Servings: 3

Nutritional Analysis:
Total Calories: 200
Total fat: 5g
Protein: 14g
Carbohydrates: 26g

Ingredients:

- 5 oz of raw shrimp
- 2 tsp of fresh coriander
- 1 tbsp of lemon juice
- 14 tsp of ground cumin
- 1/8 tsp of cayenne pepper

- 2 large burrito-sized flour tortillas
- 2 tsp of sour cream
- 2 tsp of shredded cheddar cheese with jalapenos

Instructions:

- Prepare shrimp by peeling off their shells and removing their tails. Wash and dice into manageable sizes. Remove the stems and chop the cilantro.
- Make marinade by combining cilantro, lemon juice, cumin, and cayenne pepper in a plastic bag and sealing it. Put in the shrimp, and let them marinade for 5 minutes.
- Put shrimp and marinade in a pan over medium heat. Orange shrimp should be achieved after 1–2 minutes of stir-frying. Take the shrimp out of the marinade, but don't wash the pan.
- Mix sour cream into the marinade in the skillet.
- To preheat tortillas, you may use either a big skillet or a microwave. Each tortilla should have 2 tablespoons of salsa spread upon it. Spread half of the shrimp mixture on top, then dot with cheese (one tablespoon's worth should do it).
- Sprinkle the shrimp with the sour cream marinade, using 1 tablespoon. To heat a folded tortilla, just flip it over in a skillet. Flip it over and do it again with the other tortilla, the rest of the shrimp, cheese, and marinade.
- Split each tortilla in half lengthwise. When ready to serve, sprinkle with cilantro and top with a slice of lemon.

Tacos Al Pastor (Soft Tacos with Mexican Seasoning)

Preparation Time: 30 Minutes
Servings: 2

Nutritional Analysis:
Total Calories: 229
Total fat: 14g
Protein: 9g
Carbohydrates: 19g

Ingredients:

- 5 tbsp of onion, cut
- 1.5 liters of milk
- Beef crushed into a 1-pound ball and weighed
- ½ cup of low-sodium tomato sauce
- 14 6-inch flour tortillas
- 5 tsp of shredded strong cheddar cheese
- 5 tsp of sour cream

Instructions:

- Get out the ingredients for the Mexican Seasoning and get cooking!
- Prepare the salad by dicing the onion and lettuce.
- Fry the ground beef until it's browned and then drain it. Sprinkle the spice blend and low-sodium tomato sauce over the top. Get it nice and toasty over medium heat. The tortillas should be heated.
- Use a single flour tortilla, 1/4 cup of seasoned ground beef, a teaspoon each of cheese and onion, sour cream, and lettuce, and roll up the taco.

Dish Featuring Asian Pears

Preparation Time: 20 Minutes
Servings: 1

Nutritional Analysis:
Total Calories: 271
Total fat: 13g
Protein: 16g
Carbohydrates: 11g

Ingredients:

- 2 cups of green cabbage, shredded finely
- 1 cup of red cabbage, shredded finely
- 2 scallions, chopped green and white
- 2 celery stalks, chopped
- 1 grated and seeded Asian pear
- ½ of a red bell pepper, cooked and diced
- ½ tbsp of chopped cilantro
- ¼ mug of olive oil
- 1 lime's juice
- 1 lime's worth of zest
- 1 tsp of granulated sugar

Instructions:

- Combine the green and red cabbage, onions, celery, and carrots in a large bowl.
- Chopped pear, red pepper, and fresh cilantro.
- Combine the olive oil, lime juice, lime zest, and sugar.
- Coat the cabbage salad with the dressing and toss to incorporate.
- Serve after chilling in the fridge for an hour.

Penne in a White-Only Egg Frittata

Preparation Time: 25 Minutes
Servings: 2

Nutritional Analysis:
Total Calories: 249
Total fat: 11g
Protein: 13g
Carbohydrates: 25g

Ingredients:

- 6 egg whites
- 1/3 mug soy milk
- 1 tbsp of fresh parsley, minced
- 1 tbsp of fresh thyme
- 1 tsp of fresh chives, chopped
- Cracked black pepper, just ground
- 2 tsp of olive oil
- ¼ tiny sweet onion, chopped
- 1 tsp of chopped garlic
- ½ cup red bell pepper, cooked and diced
- 2 cups of prepared pasta

Instructions:

- Get the oven up to temperature, preferably 350 °F.
- Whisk the egg whites, rice milk, parsley, thyme, and salt together in a large basin.
- Add some freshly ground black pepper and chives.
- Olive oil should be heated over medium heat in a large ovenproof pan.
- For approximately 4 minutes, or until softened, sauté the onion, garlic, and red pepper in the olive oil.
- Softened.
- Spread the cooked penne around the pan using a spatula.
- Toss the spaghetti with the egg mixture and give the pan a quick shake to evenly coat the strands.
- Let the pan sit for 1 minute to allow the frittata's base to firm.
- Toss the pan into the oven after it's been transferred.
- For a firm and golden frittata, bake it for around 25 minutes.
- Take the dish out of the oven right away and serve.

Stuffed Spaghetti Squash with Bulgur

Preparation Time: 30 Minutes
Servings: 2

Nutritional Analysis:
Total Calories: 285
Total fat: 10g
Protein: 16g
Carbohydrates: 25g

Ingredients:

- 2 halves of a tiny spaghetti squash
- 1 tsp of olive oil
- Cracked black pepper, just ground
- ½ of a tiny sweet onion, chopped
- 1 tsp of chopped garlic
- 2 cups of finely sliced carrots

- ½ mug of cranberries
- 1 tsp of fresh thyme
- ½ tsp of ground cumin
- ½ tsp of dried coriander seed
- ½ lemon's juice
- 1 cup Bulgar, ready to eat

Instructions:

- Get the oven up to temperature, preferably 350 °F.
- Put parchment paper on a baking pan.
- Squash halves should be lightly oiled, sprinkled with salt & pepper, and then placed on a baking sheet.
- Spread out on a baking sheet, cut side down.
- When the squash has baked for 25-30 minutes and is soft, take it out of the oven and turn it over.
- Take a spoon and remove the meat from each half, leaving a half an inch of skin on each side.
- Put 2 cups of the cooked squash flesh into a big bowl; set aside the remainder for later use.
- Olive oil should be heated in a medium pan over medium heat.
- For about 5–6 minutes, or until softened, sauté the onion, garlic, carrot, and cranberries.
- The sautéed veggies should be added to the squash in the bowl.
- Toss in the thyme, cumin, and coriander, and mix well.
- In a large bowl, combine the cooked bulgur and the lemon juice.
- Fill the squash halves to the same level with the filling.
- Put it in the oven and cook it for approximately 15 minutes, or until it's hot.

A Strata with Roasted Red Peppers

Preparation Time: 25 Minutes
Servings: 2

Nutritional Analysis:
Total Calories: 214
Total fat: 8g
Protein: 14g
Carbohydrates: 40g

Ingredients:

- Margarine, to coat the baking dish with
- 12 cubes of fresh white bread
- 1 tbsp of unsalted butter
- 2 medium-sized sweet onion, diced
- 1 tsp of chopped garlic
- 1 cooked and sliced red bell pepper
- 6 eggs
- ¼ cup of vinegar flavored with tarragon
- 1 cup of rice milk
- 1 tsp Tabasco pepper sauce
- ½ teaspoon of freshly ground black pepper
- 1 oz of Parmesan cheese, grated

Instructions:

- The oven temperature should be set at 250 °F.
- Prepare a 9-by-9-inch baking dish by greasing it lightly with butter.
- The bread cubes should be spread out on a baking sheet lined with parchment paper.
- Toast the cubes of bread in a preheated oven for approximately 10 minutes, or until they reach the desired crispiness.
- Take out the bread cubes and put them to the side.
- Butter should be melted in a medium pan over medium heat.
- To soften the onion and garlic, sauté them for approximately 3 minutes.
- After 2 minutes of sautéing, add the red pepper.
- Cover the bottom of the baking dish with a layer of bread cubes and then a layer of the sautéed veggies.
- To finish, use the remaining bread cubes and veggies in the same manner.
- Mix the eggs, vinegar, rice milk, spicy sauce, and pepper in a medium bowl.
- Evenly distribute the egg mixture in the baking dish.
- Soak the dish in the fridge for at least 2 hours, preferably overnight, covered.

- Relax at room temperature until the strata cool down.
- Bake at 325 degrees Fahrenheit, having preheated the oven.
- After 45 minutes, take them out of the oven and from the plastic wrap.
- To finish off the strata, sprinkle it with cheese and return to the oven for another 5 minutes.
- Prepare and serve immediately when hot.

Falafel-Style Burgers Made with Couscous

Preparation Time: 30 Minutes
Servings: 1

Nutritional Analysis:
Total Calories: 219
Total fat: 11g
Protein: 12g
Carbohydrates: 30g

Ingredients:

- 2 cup chickpeas from a can, drained and rinsed
- 2 tsp of finely chopped fresh coriander
- 2 tsp of chopped fresh parsley
- 1 tsp of lemon juice, squeezed
- 2 tsp of grated lemon peel
- 1 tsp of chopped garlic
- About 2 1/2 cups of cooked couscous
- 2 eggs, beaten gently
- 2 tbsp of olive oil

Instructions:

- To make the paste, combine the chickpeas, cilantro, parsley, lemon juice, lemon zest, and garlic in a food processor and pulse until smooth (or use a large bowl and a handheld immersion blender).
- Add the couscous and eggs to the chickpea mixture and stir until everything is well combined.
- Put the concoction in the fridge for an hour to set. Make four cakes out of the couscous mixture.
- The olive oil should be heated in a large pan set over medium heat.
- Using a spatula, push the patties down gently as you add them to the griddle in batches of two.
- back of a spoon or spatula. Turn the patties after 5 minutes of cooking time.
- Then, flip the patties and cook for another 5 minutes before transferring them to a paper towel-lined dish.
- You should do it again with the other two burgers.

Szechuan-Style Stir-Fried Tofu with Marination

Preparation Time: 20 Minutes
Servings: 3

Nutritional Analysis:
Total Calories: 216
Total fat: 10g
Protein: 16g
Carbohydrates: 40g

Ingredients:

- 1 tbsp of lemon juice, squeezed
- 1 tsp of chopped garlic
- 1 tsp of fresh ginger, grated
- Tease out some crushed red pepper
- 5 oz of extra-firm tofu, pressed and cubed
- 1 ½ tsp of olive oil
- ¼ cup broccoli florets
- ½ cup of sliced carrots
- ½ cup of julienned red pepper
- ½ cup of new green beans
- 2 cups of white rice, previously cooked

Instructions:

- Lemon juice, garlic, ginger, and crushed red pepper should be combined in a small bowl.
- Toss in the tofu to cover it with the sauce.
- Marinate for two hours in the fridge, covered.
- Warm the oil in a big pan over moderate heat.
- Sauté the tofu for 8 minutes, or until it is gently browned and cooked through.
- Through.
- Put in the cauliflower and carrots, and cook for 5 minutes while tossing and turning often.
- Cook for 3 more minutes after include the red pepper and green beans in the sauté.
- Place on the white rice.

Chapter 9: Fruits and Dessert Recipes

Granita with a sour apple flavor

Preparation Time: 10 Minutes
Servings: 1

Nutritional Analysis:
Total Calories: 209
Total fat: 16g
Protein: 6g
Carbohydrates: 30g

Ingredients:
- ½ cup of white sugar, granulated
- 10 tsp of water
- 2 glasses of pure apple juice, no sugar added
- ¼ cup of lemon juice, squeezed

Instructions:
- The sugar and water should be heated together in a small pot over medium heat.
- In a large saucepan, bring all the ingredients to a boil, then decrease the heat to low and simmer for 15 minutes, or until the liquid has reduced by half.
- Put the liquid into a big, shallow metal pan and take the pan off the heat.
- After waiting 30 minutes, add the apple juice and lemon juice and mix well.
- The dish should be chilled in the freezer.
- When ice crystals have developed after an hour, they may be broken up by stirring the liquid with a fork. You should also scrape the sides.
- To make slush, return the pan to the freezer and stir and scrape it every 20 minutes.
- When the mixture has frozen solid, after approximately 3 hours, serve it.

Topping for a Lemon-Lime Sherbet

Preparation Time: 20 Minutes
Servings: 2

Nutritional Analysis:
Total Calories: 278
Total fat: 16g
Protein: 8g
Carbohydrates: 22g

Ingredients:

- 2.5 oz of liquid
- 1 cup granulated sugar
- 3 tbsp of lemon zest, (Split)
- ½ cup of pure, unfiltered lemon juice
- 1 lime's worth of zest
- 1 lime's juice
- ½ cup of thick cream

Instructions:

- Combine the water, sugar, and 2 tablespoons of the lemon zest in a large saucepan and set it over medium heat.
- The process begins with bringing the ingredients to a boil then reducing the heat to a simmer for 15 minutes.
- Add the remaining 1 tablespoon of lemon zest, along with the lemon juice, lime zest, and lime juice, to the mixture in a large bowl.
- Put the concoction into the fridge and let it chill for three hours.
- Then, using a whisk, incorporate the heavy cream and move the mixture to an ice cream machine.
- Keep frozen as directed.

Slushy with Vanilla and Tropical Flavors

Preparation Time: 35Minutes
Servings: 2

Nutritional Analysis:
Total Calories: 266
Total fat: 10g
Protein: 9g
Carbohydrates: 38g

Ingredients:
- 1 cup canned peaches
- 1 cup of pineapple
- 1 cup of frozen strawberries
- 6 tbsp of water
- 2 tbsp of white sugar
- 1 tbsp of vanilla extract

Instructions:
- Peaches, pineapple, strawberries, water, and sugar should all be combined in a big pot and brought to a boil over medium heat.
- Bring the mixture to a simmer over low heat, stirring regularly for 15 minutes.
- Take the pot off the stove and let it cool for at least an hour.
- The fruit mixture should be transferred to a blender or food processor once the vanilla has been stirred in.
- Blend until smooth, then transfer to a glass baking dish that measures 9 by 13 inches.
- Prepare the dish the night before and store it in the freezer, covered.
- Once the fruit combination has frozen solid, scrape it with a fork to create flavorful ice flakes for your sorbet.
- Using a scoop, divide the ice into 4 individual servings.

Peach Pavlova.

Preparation Time: 25 Minutes
Servings: 2

Nutritional Analysis:
Total Calories: 271
Total fat: 10g
Protein: 11g
Carbohydrates: 40g

Ingredients:

- 12 egg whites, at room temperature
- ½ tsp of cream of tartar
- 1 cup of sugar
- ½ tsp of natural vanilla essence
- 2 cups of peaches in their juice, drained

Instructions:

- It's time to turn on the oven and set the temperature to 225 °F.
- Set aside a baking sheet that has been lined with parchment paper.
- Whites of the eggs should be beaten for approximately a minute in a large basin, or until soft peaks form.
- Cream of tartar should be beaten in.
- When the egg whites are firm and shiny, add the sugar 1 tablespoon at a time. Please don't beat it to death.
- Mix with some vanilla extract.
- Divide the meringue into 8 equal circles on the baking sheet.
- Make a divot in the centre of each circle with the back of the spoon.
- The meringues need to be baked for approximately an hour, or until a light brown crust forms.
- The meringues should be left in the off oven all night.
- Take the meringues off of the sheet and set them on plates.
- Place a spoonful of the peaches in the middle of each meringue and serve.
- Unused meringues may be kept for a week at room temperature in a sealed container.

Cinnamon Custard, a Sweet Treat

Preparation Time: 20 Minutes
Servings: 2

Nutritional Analysis:
Total Calories: 219
Total fat: 10g
Protein: 6g
Carbohydrates: 30g

Ingredients:

- Margarine, preferably unsalted butter, to coat the insides of the ramekins.
- 2 cups of plain rice milk
- 4 eggs
- ¼ cup of white sugar
- 1 tsp of vanilla extract
- ½ tsp of cinnamon powder
- To decorate, cinnamon sticks (optional)

Instructions:

- Preheat the oven to 325 °F
- Prepare a baking dish by lightly greasing six ramekins of equal size (4 ounces each).
- Mix the rice milk, eggs, sugar, vanilla, and cinnamon together in a large bowl.
- Strain the mixture into a pitcher using the fine sieve.
- Partially fill the ramekins with the custard mixture, and then divide the contents evenly among the ramekins.
- Carefully fill the baking dish with boiling water until it comes halfway up the edges of the ramekins.
- Bake for 1 hour, or until a knife inserted into the middle of one custard comes out clean, whichever comes first.
- Take the ramekins out of the water and bake the custards.
- After one hour of cooling on wire racks, move the custards to the fridge to chill for another hour.
- Sprinkle each serving of custard with cinnamon, if using.

Rhubarb Crème Brulé

Preparation Time: 25Minutes
Servings: 2

Nutritional Analysis:
Total Calories: 290
Total fat: 10g
Protein: 16g
Carbohydrates: 41g

Ingredients:
- ½ cup of light sour cream
- ½ tbsp room temperature cream cheese, plain
- ¼ cup of brown sugar, separated
- ¼ tsp of cinnamon powder
- 1 cup of fresh raspberries

Instructions:
- Turn the broiler on high.
- For approximately 4 minutes, or until the mixture is extremely thick and fluffy, beat together the sour cream, cream cheese, 2 tablespoons brown sugar, and cinnamon in a small dish.
- Put the raspberries into 4 ramekins, each holding 4 ounces.
- Evenly spread the cream cheese mixture on top of the berries.
- You may cover the ramekins and keep them in the fridge until you're ready to serve the dessert.
- Each ramekin should have a layer of brown sugar equal to about a half tablespoon.
- The ramekins should be placed on a baking sheet and broiled at a distance of 4 inches from the broiler until the sugar has caramelized and become golden.
- Put on a dish and put it in the oven. Instruct the strongest to take a seat for a minute before serving.

Couscous Pudding with a Vanilla Bean Flavoring

Preparation Time: 35 Minutes
Servings: 1

Nutritional Analysis:
Total Calories: 249
Total fat: 10g
Protein: 8g
Carbohydrates: 30g

Ingredients:
- 2 cups of plain rice milk
- 10 tsp of water
- 1 cup of a vanilla bean
- 2 cups of honey
- ¼ tsp of cinnamon powder
- 1 cup couscous

Instructions:
- Blend the rice milk, water, and vanilla bean in a large saucepan and simmer gently over medium.
- In order to infuse the milk with the vanilla flavor, bring it to a simmer over low heat and let it cook for 10 minutes.
- Take the pan off the stove immediately.
- Remove the vanilla bean and scrape the seeds with a paring knife into the milk while it is still hot.
- Combining honey and cinnamon is a nice touch.
- After adding the couscous, stir it in, cover the pan, and let it sit for 10 minutes.
- Before serving, fluff the couscous with a fork to distribute the flavor.

Baked Goods with Honey

Preparation Time: 30 Minutes
Servings: 1

Nutritional Analysis:
Total Calories: 219
Total fat: 10g
Protein: 12g
Carbohydrates: 40g

Ingredients:

- Grease a baking dish with unsalted butter.
- 2 cups of plain rice milk
- 2 eggs
- 2 big egg whites
- ¼ cup of honey
- 1 tsp of vanilla extract
- 6 cups of white bread, cubed
- Butter a square baking dish that's 8 inches by 8 inches and put it aside.

Instructions:

- The rice milk, eggs, egg whites, honey, and vanilla should all be combined in a medium bowl and whisked together.
- When ready, add the bread cubes and toss to coat.
- Put the ingredients in a baking dish and cover it with plastic.
- Put the meal in the fridge for at least three hours before serving.
- Bake at 325 degrees Fahrenheit, having preheated the oven.
- After 35-40 minutes in the oven, remove the plastic wrap from the baking dish and check the pudding with a knife to see whether it is done.
- Serve hot.

Crust with Rhubarb

Preparation Time: 20 Minutes
Servings: 1

Nutritional Analysis:
Total Calories: 270
Total fat: 10g
Protein: 9g
Carbohydrates: 30g

Ingredients:

- Grease a baking dish with unsalted butter.
- 1 cup of all-purpose flour
- 2 cups of dark sugar
- ½ tsp of cinnamon powder
- ½ cup softened unsalted butter
- 1 cup rhubarb, chopped
- 2 apples peeled and thinly sliced2 tbsp. of white sugar
- 2 tbsp of water

Instructions:

- Bake at 325 degrees Fahrenheit, having preheated the oven.
- Butter a square baking dish that's 8 inches by 8 inches and put it aside.
- In a small bowl, whisk together the flour, sugar, and cinnamon until thoroughly incorporated.
- To make coarse crumbs, add the butter and work it in with your fingertips.
- Combine rhubarb, apple, sugar, and water in a medium saucepan and stir to combine.
- For approximately 20 minutes, stirring occasionally, over medium heat, or until the rhubarb is tender.
- Fill the baking dish with the fruit mixture, then sprinkle the crumble on top.
- Allow the crumble to bake for 20 to 30 minutes, or until it reaches the desired color.
- Prepare and serve immediately when hot.

Bakery-Style Gingerbread

Preparation Time: 20 Minutes
Servings: 1

Nutritional Analysis:
Total Calories: 209
Total fat: 7g
Protein: 16g
Carbohydrates: 36g

Ingredients:

- Grease a baking dish with unsalted butter.
- 3 cups of all-purpose flour.
- 2 tsp of the baking soda
- 2 tbsp of cinnamon powder
- 1 tsp of ground allspice
- ¼ cup of granulated sugar
- ¾ cup of unsweetened rice milk
- 1 large Egg
- ¼ mug of olive oil
- 2 tbsp of molasses
- 2 tsp of grated fresh ginger
- Dusted with powdered sugar

Instructions:

- Get the oven up to temperature, preferably 350 °F.
- Put some butter in a 9-by-13-inch baking dish and put it aside.
- Mix the flour, baking powder replacement, cinnamon, and allspice in a large basin.
- Coat the flour with the sugar and stir it in.
- The milk, egg, olive oil, molasses, and ginger should be mixed together in a medium bowl using a whisk.
- The wet ingredients should be poured into a well you've made in the middle of the flour.
- Carefully blend ingredients until just mixed.
- Cook for 1 hour, or until a wooden pick inserted in the center comes out clean, after pouring the batter into the baking dish.
- Sprinkle some powdered sugar over top and serve warm.

Delicate Lavender Cookies

Preparation Time: 30 Minutes
Servings: 2

Nutritional Analysis:
Total Calories: 279
Total fat: 16g
Protein: 6g
Carbohydrates: 31g

Ingredients:

- 5 organic lavender blossoms, with the tops removed, dried
- 1/2 cup of white sugar, granulated
- 1cup of unsalted butter, room temperature
- 2 cups of all-purpose flour
- 1 cup of rice flour

Instructions:

- Carefully remove the little lavender blossoms off the main stem and add them, along with some granulated sugar, to a blender or food processor. Blend in short bursts until everything is finely chopped.
- Combine the butter and lavender sugar in a medium bowl and beat until frothy.
- Cream together the butter and sugar before adding the flours and mixing until the texture resembles fine crumbs.
- Roll the dough into a log shape after gathering it into a ball.
- Refrigerate the cookie dough for at least an hour, or until it can easily be handled.
- Get the oven up to temperature, preferably 375 °F.
- Cut the dough into rounds about 1/4 inch thick and chill it for at least an hour, or until it is solid.
- The cookies should be baked for 15–18 minutes, or until they have just a hint of golden color.
- Leave the cookies to cool.
- Cookies may be kept fresh for a week if stored in an airtight container at room temperature.

Angel Food Cake with Carob

Preparation Time: 30 Minutes
Servings: 3

Nutritional Analysis:
Total Calories: 219
Total fat: 9g
Protein: 9g
Carbohydrates: 30g

Ingredients:

- ¼ cup of all-purpose flour
- ¼ cup of carob flour
- 1 ½ cups sugar, split
- 2 large egg whites at room temperature
- 1 ½ tbsp cream of tartar

Instructions:

- Get the oven up to temperature, preferably 375 °F.
- Sift the all-purpose flour, carob flour, and 3/4 cup sugar together in a medium bowl.
- For approximately 5 minutes, or until soft peaks form, beat the egg whites and cream of tartar using a hand mixer.
- Spoon by spoon, continue adding the remaining 3/4 cup sugar to the egg whites until firm peaks form.
- Combine the flour and vanilla and fold them in.
- Fill an angel food cake pan with the batter.
- If there are any air bubbles in the batter, cut them out with a knife.
- For approximately 30 minutes, or until the top of the cake bounces back when softly touched.
- Flip the pan over onto a cooling rack.
- Use a knife to loosen the cake from the pan's edge, then lift it out.

Traditional Apple Cake

Preparation Time: 20 Minutes
Servings: 1

Nutritional Analysis:
Total Calories: 219
Total fat: 10g
Protein: 16g
Carbohydrates: 41g

Ingredients:

- Grease a baking dish with unsalted butter.
- 1 cup of unsalted butter, room temperature
- 2 mugs of white sugar crystals
- 2 beaten eggs
- 2 tsp of pure vanilla extract
- 2 cups of all-purpose flour
- 1 tsp of the baking soda
- 2 tbsp of cinnamon powder
- ½ tsp of nutmeg powder
- Crush some allspice berries
- 2 big apples, prepped by peeling, coring, and dicing (about 3 cups)

Instructions:

- Get the oven up to temperature, preferably 350 °F.
- Prepare a 9x13-inch glass baking dish with butter.
- Combine the butter and sugar in a large bowl and beat on medium speed with a hand mixer until pale and fluffy, approximately 3 minutes.
- Toss in the eggs and vanilla and beat for 1 minute, stopping to scrape down the sides of the bowl.
- Whisk together the flour, baking soda replacement, cinnamon, nutmeg, and allspice in a small basin.
- Combine the dry and wet materials by mixing them together.
- Cook the apple in the batter by stirring it in before placing it in the baking dish.
- Bake for an hour, or until the cake is brown.
- Use a wire rack to let the cake cool.
- Hot or cold, serve it whichever you want.

Flaky, Buttery Pound Cake

Preparation Time: 20 Minutes
Servings: 2

Nutritional Analysis:
Total Calories: 200
Total fat: 6g
Protein: 10g
Carbohydrates: 21g

Ingredients:

- Butter, unsalted, for use in baking
- For sprinkling the baking dish, all-purpose flour
- 2 ½ sticks of unsalted butter, softened to room temperature
- 3 cups of white sugar, granulated
- 6 eggs at room temperature
- 1 tbsp of pure vanilla extract
- 4 cups of flour, all-purpose
- ½ cup sweetened rice milk

Instructions:

- Bake at 325 °F, having preheated the oven.
- Prepare a Bundt pan, 10 inches in diameter, by greasing it with butter and then dusting it with flour.
- Cream the butter and sugar together in a large basin with a hand mixer until light and fluffy, approximately 4 minutes.
- The eggs should be added one at a time, with a thorough pounding and scraping of the bowl in between each addition.
- Mix with some vanilla extract.
- Repeat this process twice more, starting and ending with flour.
- Fill the Bundt pan with the batter.
- Cake is done when the top is golden brown and the center bounces back when softly pushed, usually about 1 hour and 15 minutes in the oven.
- Allow the cake to cool in the Bundt pan for 10 minutes before removing it from the pan.
- After removing the cake from the pan, place it on a wire rack to cool.

Yummy Apple Bars

Preparation Time: 30 Minutes
Servings: 2

Nutritional Analysis:
Total Calories: 255
Total fat: 10g
Protein: 9g
Carbohydrates: 30g

Ingredients:

- 2 apples
- ¾ cup of unsalted butter
- 1 cup of Granulated sugar
- 1 cup of sour cream
- 1 tsp of vanilla extract
- 1 tsp of baking soda

- 2 cups of all-purpose flour
- ½ cup of brown sugar
- ½ tsp of ginger
- 2 tsp of milk
- 1 cup icing sugar

Instructions:

- Prepare a 350°F oven
- Take the apples and dice them up.
- Mix the sugar and 1/2 cup of the butter until light and fluffy.
- Sour cream, vanilla, baking soda, and flour should be added. Give it a good stir, then throw in some apple chunks.
- The batter should be poured into a 9x13 pan that has been buttered.
- Mix the brown sugar, cinnamon, and the remaining 2 tablespoons of melted butter in a small bowl until the mixture resembles a crumble. Then, sprinkle them on top of the batter.
- Cook for 35–40 minutes. Leave to cool down entirely.
- Icing is made by mixing together powdered sugar, milk (or a milk substitute), and two tablespoons of melted butter. Cut the dessert into 18 bars and drizzle with the glaze.

Quick and Easy Oatmeal Muffins with Berries

Preparation Time: 30 Minutes
Servings: 2

Nutritional Analysis:
Total Calories: 219
Total fat: 9g
Protein: 7g
Carbohydrates: 35g

Ingredients:

- 1 cup of unbleached all-purpose flour
- ½ cup of instant oatmeal
- 2/3 cup of lightly packed brown sugar
- ½ tsp of baking soda
- 2 eggs
- ½ cup worth of applesauce
- ¼ cup of canola oil
- You simply need the orange's zest (from one orange)
- 1 grated lemon rind
- 1 tbsp of lemon juice
- ¾ cup of fresh or frozen raspberries
- ¾ of blueberries, fresh or frozen

Instructions:

- Place the oven rack in the center and turn on to 350°F. Prepare a muffin tin with 2 liners, either paper or silicone.
- Mix the flour, oats, brown sugar, and baking soda together in a bowl. Don't bother with right now.
- Mix the eggs, applesauce, oil, citrus zest, and lemon juice in a large bowl. The dry ingredients should be mixed in with a wooden spoon. Gently mix in the berries.
- Put heaping spoonsful into the muffin tins. The muffins are done when a toothpick put into the middle comes out clean, which should take around 20 to 22 minutes in the oven. Put aside to cool.

Fruity Drink

Preparation Time: 20 Minutes
Servings: 3

Nutritional Analysis:
Total Calories: 212
Total fat: 15g
Protein: 9g
Carbohydrates: 40g

Ingredients:

- ¼ cup of cranberry juice blend
- 2/3 cup of firm silken tofu
- ½ cup frozen raspberries, no sugar added
- ½ cup blueberries, frozen and unsweetened
- 1 tsp of vanilla extract

Instructions:

- Put some juice into the blender. Put the remaining ingredients in. Mix it up until it's silky smooth. Get it on the table right now and dig in!

Chapter 10: Smoothies and Juices Recipes

Strawberry-Banana Smoothie

Preparation Time: 30 Minutes
Servings: 2

Nutritional Analysis:
Total Calories: 219
Total fat: 10g
Protein: 16g
Carbohydrates: 30g

Ingredients:

- ½ of a banana, sliced into bits after peeling
- ½ cup of plain yogurt
- ½ tbsp of unsweetened applesauce
- ¼ cup soy, almond, or rice milk
- 1 tbsp honey
- 2 tbsp of oat or wheat bran

Instructions:

- To make a healthy smoothie, combine a banana with some yogurt, applesauce, milk, honey, and vanilla extract. Mix it up until it's a homogenous paste. To thicken, add oat bran and continue blending.

Liquid Renal Flush

Preparation Time: 30 Minutes
Servings: 1

Nutritional Analysis:
Total Calories: 219
Total fat: 11g
Protein: 10g
Carbohydrates: 36g

Ingredients:

- 1 cup of cranberries
- 4 cups of water
- 2 tbsp of date paste would enough.
- 2 red apples, peeled and sliced
- 2 lemons, squeezed
- 1 tsp cardamom (optional)
- Peppermint or mint, one organically grown sprig (optional)

Instructions:

- Bring 3 cups of water and the cranberries to a boil in a medium saucepan. Remove from heat and let cool. In a food processor, combine the remaining cup of water, the remaining 1 tablespoon of lemon juice, and the date paste. Place all the sliced apples, the cranberries, and the water in a big glass jar or container. Toss in some cardamom and mint leaves, if you like.

Blended Blueberry Blast

Preparation Time: 20 Minutes
Servings: 1

Nutritional Analysis:
Total Calories: 214
Total fat: 10g
Protein: 9g
Carbohydrates: 41g

Ingredients:

- 1 cup of blueberries, frozen
- 8 of Splenda® packets
- 6tsp of protein powder
- 8 ice cubes
- 14 oz of unsweetened apple juice

Instructions:

- Blend all the ingredients in a blender until they are completely combined.
- Protein Smoothie Made with Fresh Pineapple
- 1/4 cup frozen pineapple juice 3/4 cup sherbet or sorbet
- A single serving of vanilla flavored whey protein powder
- Approximately one-half cup of water
- Add 2 ice cubes if desired
- Put some pineapple sherbet, protein powder, and water in a blender (ice cubes optional).
- Do not delay; combine for 30–45 seconds at once.

Smoothie Made with Blueberries and Pineapple.

Preparation Time: 28 Minutes
Servings: 1

Nutritional Analysis:
Total Calories: 221
Total fat: 16g
Protein: 10g
Carbohydrates: 19g

Ingredients:
- 1 cup of blueberries, frozen
- ½ cup of pineapple slices
- 1/2 cup of chopped English cucumber
- ½ apple
- 10 tsp of water

Instructions:
- Simply combine the blueberries, pineapple, cucumber, apple, and water in a blender and process until smooth.
- Mix until it becomes thick and creamy.
- Serve immediately in two glasses.

Strawberry-Watermelon Smoothie

Preparation Time: 25 Minutes
Servings: 2

Nutritional Analysis:

- Total Calories: 210
  Total fat: 10g
  Protein: 8g
  Carbohydrates: 21g

  Ingredients:

- ½ cup red cabbage that has been cooked, chilled, and shredded
- 1 cup watermelon, chopped
- ¼ pound frozen blueberries

Instructions:

- In a cup of ice to finely chop the cabbage, place it in a blender and process for 2 minutes.
- In a food processor, mix the watermelon and raspberries and pulse for 1 minute.
- Blend the ice into the smoothie until it reaches a thick and smooth consistency.
- Serve immediately in two glasses.

Chapter 11: The 30-Day Meal Plan

Day	Breakfast	Lunch	Snack	Dinner	Dessert
1	A Blend of Apples and Chai	Pizzeria's Famous Grilled Chicken Pita Pizza	Dip with Roasted Onion and Garlic	Herb and Lemon Chicken	Blended Blueberry Blast
2	Smoothie made with Blueberries and Pineapple.	The Brewery's Burger	Baba Ghanoush	Satay Chicken from Asia	Liquid Renal Flush
3	Strawberry-Watermelon Smoothie	Nachos With Crunchy Chicken	Herb-and-Cheese Spread	Curry Chicken	Strawberry-Banana Smoothie
4	Fruity Holiday Parfait	Quesadillas with Camarones	Fried Kale Chips with a Kick	Spiced Chicken from India	Fruity Drink
5	Breakfast Hot Cereal with a Variety of Grains	Tacos Al Pastor (Soft Tacos with Mexican Seasoning)	Tortilla Chips with Cinnamon	Spicy Chicken from Iran	Quick and Easy Oatmeal Muffins with Berries
6	Creme de Maze	Beef Rollups in Tortillas (High Protein)	Gourmet Kettle Corn with a Sweet and Spicy Coating	Pork Chops with Pesto	Yummy Apple Bars

Day	Breakfast	Lunch	Snack	Dinner	Dessert
7	Bread Pudding with Rhubarb	Salad with Waldorf Dressing and Turkey	Ice Pops with Blueberries and Cream	Succulent Pork Souvlaki	Flaky, Buttery Pound Cake
8	Muffins Flavored with Cinnamon and Nutmeg Studded with Blueberries.	Balsamic Vinaigrette-Dressed Lettuce and Carrot Salad	Candy Ginger with Frozen Milk	Pork Legs with Chili Rub	Traditional Apple Cake
9	Snack Wrap with Fruit and Cheese for the Morning Meal	Strawberry Watercress Salad with Almond Dressing	Delicious Meringue Cookies	Pan-Seared Beef Stir-Fry	Angel Food Cake with Carob
10	Egg-In-The-Hole	Salsa with Limón	Crostini With Roasted Red Peppers, Chicken, And Feta	Meatloaf with a Sweet and Sour Sauce	Delicate Lavender Cookies

Day	Breakfast	Lunch	Snack	Dinner	Dessert
11	Delicious Pancakes	Salad with Asparagus and Leaf Lettuce with Raspberries	Vegetables in Cucumber Wraps	Steak With a Cool and Citrusy Salsa Made from Cucumbers and Cilantro on the Grill	Bakery-Style Gingerbread
12	French Toast Stuffed with Strawberries and Cream Cheese	Salad Waldorf	Antojitos	Traditional Pot Roast	Crust with Rhubarb
13	A Blend of Apples and Chai	Dish Featuring Asian Pears	Skewers with Chicken and Veggies	Calamari with Herbs and Lemon, Grilled	Baked Goods with Honey
14	Smoothie made with Blueberries and Pineapple.	Salad of Couscous and Vegetables Dressed with a Spicy Citrus Dressing.	Lettuce Wraps with Five Spice Chicken	Tuna with Pesto and Herbs	Couscous Pudding with a Vanilla Bean Flavoring
15	Fruity Holiday Parfait	Confetti Salad with Farfalle	Dip with Roasted Onion and Garlic	Fish with Cilantro and Lime	Rhubarb Crème Brulé

Day	Breakfast	Lunch	Snack	Dinner	Dessert
16	Breakfast Hot Cereal with a Variety of Grains	Tabbouleh	"Baba Ghanoush"	Sole Fillets	Cinnamon Custard, a Sweet Treat
17	Bread Pudding with Rhubarb	Lemon Gratings One	Herb-and-Cheese Spread	Beef Stew, Roasted	Peach Pavlova.
18	Muffins Flavored with cinnamon and nutmeg, studded with blueberries	Salad with Ginger Beef	Fried Kale Chips with a Kick	Soup with Ground Beef and Rice	Slushy with Vanilla and Tropical Flavors
19	Snack Wrap with Fruit and Cheese for the Morning Meal	Penne in a White-Only Egg Frittata	Tortilla Chips with Cinnamon	Soup with Bulgur and Turkey	Topping for a Lemon-Lime Sherbet
20	Egg-In-The-Hole	Cooked Rice with Vegetables	Gourmet Kettle Corn with a Sweet and Spicy Coating	Hot Grain Cereal	Granita with a Sour Apple Flavor

Day	Breakfast	Lunch	Snack	Dinner	Dessert
21	Delicious Pancakes	Stuffed Spaghetti Squash with Bulgur	Gourmet Kettle Corn with a Sweet and Spicy Coating	Kebabs With Beef and Vegetables	Granita with a Sour Apple Flavor
22	A Blend of Apples and Chai	A Strata with Roasted Red Peppers	Candy Ginger with Frozen Milk	Spicy Breasts of Chicken	Topping for a Lemon-Lime Sherbet
23	Fruity Holiday Parfait	Falafel-Style Burgers Made with Couscous	Delicious Meringue Cookies	Herb and Lemon Chicken	Slushy with Vanilla and Tropical Flavors
24	French Toast Stuffed with Strawberries and Cream Cheese	Szechuan-Style Stir-Fried Tofu with Marination	Crostini With Roasted Red Peppers, Chicken, And Feta	Satay Chicken from Asia	Peach Pavlova
25	Smoothie made with Blueberries and Pineapple.	Vegetable Curry with a Thai Twist	Vegetables in Cucumber Wraps	Curry Chicken	Cinnamon Custard, a Sweet Treat

Day	Breakfast	Lunch	Snack	Dinner	Dessert
26	Delicious Pancakes	Sauce Made from Roasted Red Peppers and Basil Served Over Linguine	Rice That Has Been Fried	Pork Chops with Pesto	Rhubarb Crème Brulé
27	Bread Pudding with Rhubarb	Recipe for Baked Macaroni and Cheese	Skewers with Chicken and Veggies	Succulent Pork Souvlaki	Couscous Pudding with a Vanilla Bean Flavoring
28	Breakfast Hot Cereal with a Variety of Grains	Fried Egg and Grilled Kale Sandwich	Lettuce Wraps with Five Spice Chicken	Pork Legs with Chili Rub	Baked Goods with Honey
29	Strawberry-Watermelon Smoothie	Eggplant and Tofu Stir-Fry	Dip with Roasted Onion and Garlic	Pan-Seared Beef Stir-Fry	Crust with Rhubarb
30	Breakfast Hot Cereal with a Variety of Grains	Recipe for Broccoli and Meatball Mie Goreng	Herb-and-Cheese Spread	Meatloaf with a Sweet and Sour Sauce	Bakery-Style Gingerbread

CONCLUSION

You've made it to the final page of the book; please accept my congratulations. I put every fibre of my being into this work. Therefore, it is crucial for the dialysis patient's well-being to keep electrolyte, mineral, and fluid levels in a state of equilibrium. Only with the blessing of your primary care physician should you make the switch to a low-protein, kidney-friendly diet.

Your doctor will instead give you kudos for being proactive in managing your renal problem. Remember that not comprehending the advice of medical experts is never a valid excuse for ignoring such advice. Kidney function steadily and gradually decreases in those with chronic renal failure, also known as chronic kidney disease. When the kidneys aren't functioning properly, they may still be able to filter out some of the harmful substances in the blood, but the condition is made worse by the body's tendency to retain fluid. Even if the kidneys have the ability to filter out harmful substances, this will nonetheless occur. When the body swells to dangerous proportions, breathing becomes more difficult, and the pulse rate speeds up.

The kidneys, in a healthy organism, will process any surplus fluid and excrete it. However, if one kidney is injured or sick, this process may be hampered, leading to a potentially fatal situation. Avoiding this disease can need nothing more than stringent dietary restrictions or switching to a renal diet. It helps regulate the buildup of waste materials in the blood and reduces stress on the kidneys. In order to improve renal function, the following changes are advised for the renal diet: Taking salt out of one's diet may reduce the strain on the kidneys and protect them from injury. A healthy person's diet should not contain pig, beef, cured meats, bacon, sausages, cheese, pickles, Chinese food, or soy. Avoid canned foods, especially those containing processed or preserved meats, vegetables, or seafood. Naturally low-sodium meals include wild-caught fish and grass-fed beef.

Made in the USA
Las Vegas, NV
04 June 2023

72951985R00072